putting children first

A handbook for separated parents

Karen and Nick Woodall

PIATKUS

PIATKUS

First published in Great Britain in 2007 by Piatkus
Reprinted 2007, 2008, 2009 (twice)

Copyright © 2007 by Karen Woodhall and Nick Woodhall

The moral right of the author has been asserted.

All rights reserved.
No part of this publication may be reproduced, stored in a
retrieval system, or transmitted in any form or by any means,
without the prior permission in writing of the publisher, nor
be otherwise circulated in any form of binding or cover other
than that in which it is published and without a similar
condition including this condition being imposed on the
subsequent purchaser.

A CIP catalogue record for this book is available
from the British Library

ISBN 978-0-7499-2804-9

Printed and bound in Great Britain by
CPI Antony Rowe, Chippenham, Wilts

Papers used by Piatkus are natural, renewable and recyclable
products sourced from well-managed forests and certified
in accordance with the rules of the Forest Stewardship Council.

Mixed Sources
Product group from well-managed
forests and other controlled sources
www.fsc.org Cert no. SGS-COC-004081
© 1996 Forest Stewardship Council
FSC

Piatkus
An imprint of
Little, Brown Book Group
100 Victoria Embankment
London EC4Y 0DY

An Hachette UK Company
www.hachette.co.uk

www.piatkus.co.uk

Contents

7. Our final thoughts 262

To Laura, Joe and Hannah

Acknowledgements

We would like to acknowledge the following people for their contribution to bringing this book to fruition: Liz Savage who developed and delivered our Children in Focus courses to mothers and fathers in York; Steve Millett for his academic stringency in furthering our ideas about parenting after family separation; Fiona Hubbard for her belief in our work and continued support of our determination to put our ideas to a wider audience; Jack O'Sullivan for his positive encouragement and support; District Judge Peter Wildsmith for his belief in the importance of mothers and fathers in their children's lives after family separation; Sue Smith and Julie Jarman from Oxfam UK for their encouragement and belief in our vision; staff at the Centre for Separated Families, past and present, who work tirelessly to deliver much needed support to mothers and fathers who are struggling to cooperate after separation; Piatkus Books for recognising that mothers and fathers need extra help during family separation; and to LR, LB and LN for their company during the writing of this book.

Introduction

This book is based upon a parenting support programme called Children in Focus that was developed at the Centre for Separated Families over a period of two years. The Centre was set up for the purpose of supporting parents who are separated to build cooperative parenting relationships for the well-being of their children. When we began this work it was difficult to convince people that it was possible to help separated parents to work together. Over time we have found that far from being impossible to support parents to work together, it is actually very easy. This is because away from the feelings of grief, sadness, anger and blame, most parents want to keep close contact with their children and want to enjoy the day-to-day life that they shared before the relationship with their partner changed.

As co-authors of the Children in Focus courses, we are aware that it is not always possible to devote time to attending courses however useful they may be. Over time, though, we have become more aware of the positive impact that Children in Focus can have on the long-term well-being of children.

We have, therefore, written this book so that you can use the techniques and strategies from the Children in Focus course and apply them to your own lives at your own pace. By reading this book you can take your time to think about the information given, try out the exercises and, we hope, find the support that you need. Ideally both parents will read this book along with grandparents and other interested family members. When we run Children in Focus courses we like each parent to attend although we don't expect parents to attend on the same night!

The idea is that if each parent is learning about each other's experience and about the needs of their children, a greater empathy and understanding can develop between you. It may seem impossible at first, especially in the early days when feelings are running high, but in the long term it is worth it for your children's sake. You may never want to speak to your ex-partner again, but your children are a different matter.

This book is based upon our beliefs that children living in separated families fare best when they have close contact with each of their parents and all of the important adults in their lives, including grandparents, cousins, aunts and uncles, and family friends.

We also believe that arrangements for time spent with each parent and their families should be relaxed and as informal as possible, remaining flexible and responsive to children's changing needs. What a child wants and needs at the age of two is not what a child wants and needs at the age of 12. We base our beliefs on our own personal experience of bringing up children as separated parents and on the wide range of research[*] that shows the benefits to children of ongoing relationships with both mothers and fathers.

Children in Focus starts from a child-centred perspective, which means understanding how children are feeling and how they experience the situation. Understanding your children's perspective will help to underline the importance of

[*] Rogers and Pryor, 'Divorce & Separation: the Outcomes for Children'. Report for the Joseph Rowntree Foundation, 1998.

working cooperatively with your ex. It won't always be easy and you may find some of the ideas in this book are very different from your own, but all have been tried and tested with real families over the past two decades and have shown to have a powerfully positive influence on the children involved.

This book is written from our own experience, both as parents and as family counsellors and trainers. All of the personal stories in the book come from real-life experiences; some of them are based on our own lives, and occasionally advice from children affected by conflict in family separation is included. We feel it is important that the voices of children affected by family separation are heard, particularly because it is they who are so deeply affected by conflict between parents.

This book isn't meant to teach you how to be a parent; you know that already and have done a good-enough job until now. Its purpose is to help you to understand family separation from the perspective of children and to understand that while your adult relationship may have ended, your parenting relationship has not.

As separated parents ourselves we believe that the role of mothers and fathers is both to care and provide for their children. We do not subscribe to the belief that children 'belong' with their mother and that fathers should simply pay their child support.

We firmly believe that children living in separated family situations want and need close and loving contact with mothers and fathers and that, where possible, sharing this on a regular basis is beneficial to children. We do not believe, however, that children's time should be divided into two like the possessions or the house when a relationship ends. Children may adapt to spending half of the week with one parent and half with the other, but most children appreciate a little flexibility within the arrangements made.

The most important thing for children is that they are not made to feel as though their parents are competing for their favour or that the other parent will be upset if arrangements are changed. Young children respond well to firm and clear arrangements that are consistent throughout; teenagers, however, will eventually rebel against this if they are not given space to express their own needs and desires.

Our aim is to show you that with a little time and pause for thought, a willingness to accept the importance of the children's other parent in their lives and the motivation to keep trying, your separated family life can be arranged for the benefit of everyone involved.

Before you start on this journey, however, you must be aware that reaching this goal requires some self-awareness and a willingness to challenge some of the ways in which you think about yourself as a parent. If being a mother means caring full-time for your children and meeting their every need, this book will be a challenge. If being a father simply means paying your child support or playing with and disciplining your children, there is little in this book to support that.

Gender roles are challenged throughout this book and the ways that we think about being a good mum or a good dad are also addressed and challenged. Being a good enough separated mum or dad means being prepared to do some of the caring and some of the providing, and finding ways to support your children's other parent to do the same. In the early days of the twenty-first century, we feel it's time we all shared the responsibility for bringing up the next generation.

Perhaps the hardest thing for separated parents to do, particularly fathers, who find it hard to get the kind of daily contact with their children they would like, is to let go of any notions of parental rights. This book is not about how to achieve your rights in relationship to your children, it is about how to build a cooperative relationship with your ex-partner that understands your children's changing needs and meets these as far as possible.

We believe that taking the 'rights' based approach does not help children in the long run, because they end up feeling as if their needs are secondary to those of their parents. Sometimes it is necessary to resort to the Family Courts to settle entrenched conflict about arrangements for care of your children; even in these circumstances we think this book can help by offering you ideas and strategies for changing your behaviour and addressing the issues that give rise to conflict. In the most entrenched conflicts that we have worked with we have found that what lies at the heart of them is a lack of trust, as well as unresolved anger and grief. By working through this book, and, perhaps, giving a copy of it to your ex-partner, you should be able to address some of the issues and make small changes that will lead to a better level of trust between the two of you. Whatever your circumstances, we hope this book helps you to move away from conflict and towards a greater degree of cooperation.

Some of the exercises in the book may not be useful; if this is the case, turn the page and move on. Some of the advice may not be relevant to your situation, if so, ignore it. What we want to do is offer you a sense of being understood and an idea of how to deal with some of the big issues you will be facing as a separated mother or father. This book is meant to be used almost like a recipe book, read the bits that are relevant to you and your situation and use them as often as possible.

However you use the book, we would like to hear from you

if you find it useful, and if you feel that something is missing that would have helped you more, please let us know. You will find the address for the Centre for Separated Families along with our website address in Resources, at the end of the book. Good luck, we hope this book makes a difference to your separated family.

Chapter 1

All About You

'The world has shattered into a thousand pieces and everything that I trusted about life has fallen apart. Not only that, but the person who is making life this bad is the person who always made my life better. I don't know which way to turn.'
Jill – mother to three boys, two weeks after her husband left home

IF YOU RECOGNISE those feelings you are probably the person who has been left in a relationship. For many people in this situation the ending is sudden and often unexplained and can be very difficult to come to terms with.

Relationships end for lots of different reasons, as many reasons as there are different ways of having a relationship. Perhaps you have been married for some time, or living together, or perhaps you have been partners who live in separate homes.

How you lived out your relationship will affect how you experience the end of it and how you recover from the massive physical, emotional and mental change that such an ending brings about.

The end of a relationship is the second most stressful event in our lives; it is second only to the death of a spouse or partner. When a relationship ends there are many different feelings to deal with and a period of adjustment that cannot be avoided. Many people talk of feeling as though they want to run away from their feelings at this time; the pain is too great to bear and the grief is too overwhelming.

It is important to understand what is happening to you at this time because when you understand the psychological processes, it is possible to see the road ahead more clearly. By doing so, you will see that the pain will become more bearable. This understanding can give you the courage and hope that helps to keep you functioning throughout the early days.

If you are the person who is left in a relationship it can feel shocking as well as frightening and overwhelming. If you did not have any inkling that the end was coming, the shock can feel impossible to cope with.

If you have been left in a relationship and you are reading this in the early days or weeks afterwards, you may still be feeling disbelief, numb or as though you are waiting for your partner to come home again. Being left in a relationship can produce feelings and sensations that are very close to those of bereavement and it is important that you understand the impact of such a shock on your physical, mental and emotional well-being. Now is the time to learn about taking good care of yourself, if you don't already. Some of the ways in which you can start to do that, even in the first days after a break-up, can be found later in this chapter.

When relationships end, it is always an enormous task to come to terms with what has happened. When your relationship ends and your children are involved, it is an even greater task because while you are coping with the impact on your own life, you are also expected to be coping with the effects on your children.

Relationships, however, don't suddenly come apart at the seams. It is unlikely that someone will wake up one morning and decide to leave a relationship on the spur of the moment. For everyone, leaver and left, there are processes that occur in relationships and there is always a period of subtle or not so subtle change.

'In my mind I was working out how to tell him that I didn't want to live with him any more, that it was over for me. But then I would see him with Charlie our littlest boy and I would put it to one side again, I couldn't see how I could do it to Charlie, even if I could do it to him.'

Suzanne – mother to Zeb aged ten and Charlie aged three

If those words from Suzanne resonate with you then you are probably the person who has left the relationship. Your experience is likely to be different to that of the other person, but it doesn't mean that it will necessarily be easier. For those who leave, there are different feelings to cope with and these often run side by side so that it can be confusing and difficult to understand what you are feeling or why. Feelings of guilt can run alongside feelings of relief, or a new sense of freedom and purpose might be tinged with feelings of sadness and nostalgia.

The emotional work and tasks of grieving that come with the end of a relationship are hard work for the leaver and the left. The leaver, however, might find themselves without much support, or facing a lot of hostile feelings within the family or circle of friends. Whereas it might be a good feeling to have made the change, especially if you have been thinking about it for some time, you may have been unprepared for the reactions of other people or your own.

If you are the person who has left the relationship, your

children and your family home, a sense of dislocation and disorientation will almost certainly be present. Your adjustment to the change may take equally as long as the person who is left behind, and at the same time as coping with this, you are expected to cope with your children's feelings and how the change affects them.

The leaver and the left

'When a relationship breaks up ... the worst that happens to the leaver is a little survivor guilt.'
Woody Allen in *Everyone Says I Love You* (1997)

How we experience the end of a relationship will depend upon whether we are the person who has instigated the ending or not. Throughout this chapter we refer to the person who instigates the ending as the leaver and the other person as the left.

It is important, for the purposes of building a cooperative parenting relationship after separation, that each person understands and deals with the issues that arise from the ending of a relationship, and that each person understands what the other is likely to be experiencing.

When there is a high level of understanding about how the other person feels, communication about children becomes easier. When each person can make allowances, can compromise and can continue to respect their ex-partner, cooperation becomes possible.

It is important to get clear in your mind that the ending of a relationship takes up a lot of emotional energy, regardless of whether you are the leaver or the left.

Do not expect simply to be able to throw off the habits of

your old life, even if a new and seemingly more exciting life awaits you, especially when you have children. Endings take time and If you are to avoid creating a situation where your children fear that your relationship with them is ending too, you must give yourself enough time to deal with the change step by step. In this way, you will offer your children the security that they need so that they will experience what is happening as change rather than an ending.

Dealing with feelings

To build a cooperative relationship with your ex-partner it is necessary to deal with what you are feeling about the ending of your relationship with them. What you feel will change as time passes and it is useful to learn the techniques of under-standing your feelings and recognising where you are in the process of psychological change that accompanies the ending of your relationship.

THE LEAVER

If you are the leaver you are likely to be experiencing some or all of the following feelings:

- Guilt

- Relief

- Excitement

- Sadness

- Anxiety

- Disorientation

- Shame

- Determination

- Happiness

- Grief

However, you may not recognise any of these feelings or you may feel only some of them. Sometimes feelings can seem jumbled so that it is difficult to know what you are feeling at any given time. Learning how to decipher your feelings can help you in the long run, however, because by recognising how you feel it is possible to make clear choices and decisions. It is also easier to communicate these to your ex-partner. It is also useful to know how you feel so that you are in a better position to deal with your ex-partner's reactions to what has happened.

The following table can help you to work out your feelings:

Feeling	How it affects your mood	How it affects your body	Why do you feel it?
Guilt	Feeling low or depressed, anxious thoughts about ex-partner and children.	Fatigue, limbs feeling heavy, sleep disturbance, lack of concentration.	Psychological and emotional ties to ex-partners remain even though the relationship has ended.
Relief	Ability to concentrate improved, feeling happier and clear in mind.	Feeling as though a weight has been lifted from shoulders, sleep improves.	The fear of facing the consequences of leaving has been removed.

Feeling	How it affects your mood	How it affects your body	Why do you feel it?
Anxiety	Repetitive thoughts, lack of concentration.	Headaches, neck tension, dry mouth and throat.	Change of routine caused by leaving, uncertainty about the future.
Shame	Self-criticism, feelings of failure and worthlessness.	Tearfulness, agoraphobia, stomach upsets.	We have been brought up not to hurt other people and have transgressed this rule.
Grief	Overwhelming sensation of loss, crying periods, absentmindedness.	Tight feeling in chest, stomach in knots, headaches.	We are coping with the loss of our hopes and beliefs about the life we have left.

If you are the leaver, it is important to realise that you are in a very different place both emotionally and physically to your ex-partner. On an emotional level, you are probably feeling a sense of relief from the dread of having to tell your ex-partner that you are leaving. If you have been in another relationship for some time, you may feel exhilaration that you are now able to spend as much time with this person as you wish to.

If you have left your ex-partner because of difficulties in the relationship – domestic abuse or long-standing arguments and unhappiness – you will be feeling a range of things: relief, anxiety, perhaps some fear. If you are in these circumstances, try to make sure that you have as many people around you as possible to support you through the early days.

Having left the relationship, your children may have accompanied you to live in a new home. You may be living in a refuge or other safe house or you may have left your children with your ex-partner. Whatever situation you find yourself in, it is important that you remember that it is you who has left the relationship behind, not your children. You may never want to see your ex-partner again, but that does not mean that your children feel the same way about their other parent. In the midst of your feelings, in the early days of the break-up of your relationship, it is important to consider how you will see your children regularly, or, if they are living with you, how they will see their other parent regularly.

If you are the person who has left a relationship, be prepared for a wide range of reactions from your ex-partner. Try to keep communication channels open, utilising, if possible, friends and family to make arrangements for children to see both of you. Be prepared for anger and rejection and, at first, high levels of hostility and perhaps some acts of 'revenge'.

THE LEFT

Being left in a relationship is incredibly difficult to deal with, especially if there are new partners on the scene. Feeling betrayed, at the same time as trying to cope with the loss of a partner, is, perhaps, one of the most difficult emotional tasks to deal with. If you are the leaver, you cannot expect your ex-partner to feel like being cooperative in the early days. But with patience and a willingness to understand and accept your ex-partner's feelings of grief, anger and sadness, you can ensure that in time, the ground is prepared for coop-eration between the two of you.

If you are the person who has been left in a relation-ship and the ending seemed to come out of the blue, you are unlikely to be able to feel anything for some time because the shock will trigger a numb sensation, often accompanied by an inability to believe that this has happened to you. This numb feeling is your body's way of protecting you from becoming overwhelmed with the intense feelings that come with the shock of being left alone by someone that you love.

If you had an inkling that the ending was coming you may already have moved along from feeling numb and be experi-encing some anger or sadness. Generally speaking, being left in a relationship is very close to the experience of bereave-ment, where the person left behind has a number of 'tasks of grieving' to complete.

It is considered normal for it to take a period of around two years for these tasks to be completed and the loss accepted and incorporated into everyday life. When you have been left in a relationship, particularly if the ending came out of the blue or the ending has involved your partner moving into another relationship, it is important that you accept the need to grieve and get the support and help that you need to do so.

The Change Curve*

In our work with parents at the Centre for Separated Families, we have found that helping people to understand

* With thanks to Elizabeth Kuhbler Ross.

the emotional and psychological processes that accompany separation is important. Many parents, whether they have been the leaver or the left, tell us that the following map, called the Change Curve, is useful because it gives an idea of what to expect in the weeks and months after the ending of a relationship.

A psychologist called Elizabeth Kuhbler Ross, who spent a lot of time working with terminally ill people and their relatives, developed the Change Curve, which became a tool that is widely used in helping people to deal with grief after bereavement. We have found that it is also helpful in working with people who are coming to terms with family separation.

The Change Curve shows the stages of emotional and psychological change that we progress through after family separation, or indeed any great change in our lives, such as moving house or changing jobs. The idea is that in order to integrate fully the change that has happened in our lives, we will experience some or all of the stages shown.

Finally, when we have moved through the stages, we find ourselves back on an even keel. It is not as though the change or event never happened, but rather that we have found a way of coping and have accepted it. In most cases, we will also have changed our thinking and our behaviour as a result of the change and will find that the things we have learned in the process of the change will stand us in good stead for any future life changes that we choose or have imposed upon us.

Try to locate where you might be on the Change Curve as you are reading this.

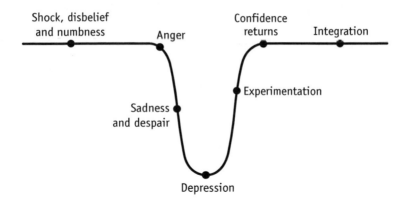

Each stage of the Change Curve relates to an emotional or psychological state through which most people pass after family separation. The rate at which someone passes through the changes will depend on many things: the length of the relationship, the level of trust and intimacy in the relationship, whether the ending was foreseen or not, whether anyone else is involved in the ending and, most importantly, whether two people have children together.

The process of coping with loss and change is not necessarily linear and not everyone goes through each stage. Most people will find that they are moving from one state to another and back again throughout the first months after the break-up of a relationship.

Children of parents who are separating will also go through some or all of the changes shown and it can be useful to try to identify where children might be on the curve. Helping children to understand that what they are feeling is normal after family separation, and that change is not always a bad thing, will help them to feel less frightened and more in control of their feelings and their environment.

Too often conflict can arise because two people cannot communicate what they are feeling effectively. This can be exacerbated by the fact that each person in the relationship that has ended is feeling different things and is on a different place on the Change Curve.

By understanding where each family member is on the Change Curve, you can have a good idea of what to expect in your own and everyone else's behaviour. This reduces the sense of chaos that family separation can create and helps to place some control back into your hands as parents.

Shock, disbelief and numbness

This is the first stage of change, and in the case of family separation it is brought about by the ending of a familiar way of life and the absence of your partner. The shock of this stage can release an overwhelming cocktail of chemicals and hormones into your body, an intense mixture that gives rise to what is often called the 'fight or flight' syndrome. This physical state is a leftover from the days when we were living closer to the land, when our physical existence depended upon us being able to defend ourselves against predators or survive in a crisis situation.

'Fight or flight' syndrome is produced by the release of adrenalin, which enables us to deal with anything that we feel may threaten us. Adrenalin (epinephrine) rushes through the body along with other chemicals, such as nor-adrenalin (norepinephrine), which contributes to an increase in physical strength and a sensitivity to noise, smells and other perceived dangers. When you are in this state of being, it can be impossible to sleep because of the combination of high-alert hormones in your body. You may feel exhausted but unable to stop moving, images may rush around your mind repeatedly or you may feel restless and extremely anxious.

This state of being puts an enormous strain on your body

because of your inability to sleep and rest properly. It is essential at this time to find ways of letting yourself rest whenever you can. A ten-minute nap can be enough to restore your energy levels again. When you have children to care for, however, it can be difficult to get this time for yourself; one of the good reasons for making sure that your children are spending plenty of time with their other parent.

USEFUL THINGS TO DO IN THE FIRST STAGES

All of the following can help you when you are in the first stages of shock after family separation. Remember that this is the emergency stage and it won't last for ever, but you may find it extremely difficult. Nonetheless, it is essential to take good care of yourself. By caring for yourself you are making it easier to care for your children.

Eating and drinking: Try to stick to regular, easily digestible meals. In this stage your body has reduced your digestive function to a minimum to conserve energy to deal with the perceived threat. You may not even feel hungry at all, but making small meals at regular intervals and sitting down quietly to eat them will help to even out the hormones and reduce anxiety and restlessness. Good foods to eat during this stage are:

- Oats with milk and honey – which are calming and soothing to the nervous system.

- Homemade soups – warming and nutritious. Use sweet potatoes, carrots and parsnips in winter, and beetroot, peas and lettuce in summer. All of these vegetables are high in natural vitamins and minerals and will therefore support your body. Chopping and slicing vegetables can also have a calming effect on your mind.

- Wholemeal breads, pasta and wholegrain rice – small amounts at a time so as not to put too much demand on the digestive system. These ensure that the body has a regular supply of slow-burning carbohydrate, which is essential for balanced hormone levels in your body.

- Fruit juices, spring water, green tea and herbal teas. All of these keep you hydrated and do not add to the stress levels in your body.

All of the above are the best foods to eat to help your body to cope with the high levels of stress you are experiencing. If your normal diet, however, looks nothing like this, we are certainly not advocating that you switch to it immediately! The main thing to keep in mind is that the foods listed are those that are supportive to a body with high levels of stress.

If you normally eat a high-sugar, high-fat diet, try to replace just one meal with one of the suggestions above and, if you do nothing else, try to keep your tea and coffee intake to a minimum. Not easy when you are in crisis we know, but the caffeine in tea and coffee serves to massively increase the levels of stress hormones in your body, making you even more exhausted. Other things to avoid when you are in this stage are milk chocolate and too many processed foods. These are high in sugar and can contribute to mood swings and exhaustion.

Whatever you do in the first stages after family separation, however, we do not recommend drinking alcohol to excess and we especially recommend that you do not drink alcohol alone. This is because alcohol releases inhibitions, which at this stage can mean that some overwhelming feelings are released. It is not uncommon for people at this point to find themselves crying uncontrollably or raging furiously. Some people who drink during this period are prone to acts of 'revenge' or to ringing up their ex-partner to tell them exactly what they think of them.

One of the best pieces of advice we can give to parents who are in this stage of the Change Curve comes from one of the parents we worked with many years ago. This parent took to drinking red wine during the first week after her husband left her for another woman and, in a fit of anger after a couple of glasses, she cut her husband's collection of silk ties in half. This parent paid dearly for her act of revenge in the divorce court when her ex-partner was awarded a cool £4,000 to replace the ties his ex-wife had literally severed. Speaking about her experience, this parent said:

> 'During the day I was fine, well as fine as you can be when you are coping with three children alone after your husband has left home. But in the evenings I had a couple of drinks to help me to calm down. One evening, after a particularly difficult day, I had a couple more than usual, thinking that it would relax me more. Unfortunately it had the opposite effect and I found all of the pent-up feelings of rage just rushed out. Cutting the ties was something I did on the spur of the moment, in a fit of rage and fury at his betrayal of our relationship. In the morning I couldn't believe I had done it and just sat and looked at this pile of ties cut into two neat pieces on the bedroom floor. I found myself crying with hopelessness and despair and everything just washed over me. I don't think I functioned properly after that for months and months.'

Shock and the accompanying disbelief and numbness have a purpose, which is to protect us from the huge waves of feeling that we cannot yet bear. Alcohol can cut through this protective layer and can act to release these feelings prematurely, plunging us into a maelstrom of despair and hopelessness. The advice from Terri, whose story is quoted above, is:

'If you must drink alcohol, do so carefully and sensibly and, above all, try to avoid drinking too much alone while you are in this stage. A couple of glasses of wine with a meal and a friend by your side is fine but make sure that alcohol isn't something that you turn to as a comfort blanket or crutch to get you through this stage. The results can be devastating because you may find yourself becoming overwhelmed with negative feelings that can take months and maybe years to deal with.'

Anger

The second stage of the Change Curve is, for some people, the most terrifying stage of all. If you have grown up feeling afraid of anger, in other people as well as yourself, this stage can feel as if you are out of control. Some parents have described this stage to us as feeling as though they are going crazy. Sometimes it can be fear of anger that creates the sensation of losing control or going crazy, because we try to suppress the feeling or change it into something else.

Anger is a difficult subject for us to deal with in our culture because it is one of the emotions we are taught to suppress as children. Young children, particularly those who are two years old, express their anger easily and freely, stamping their feet with rage if they do not get their own way or screaming until they are red in the face.

Unfortunately, for most of us, by the time we reach adulthood we are unable to express our rage and anger in healthy ways. Anger is a natural emotion and its discharge can leave us feeling cleansed and with much reduced levels of tension. Sadly, most of us have learned to keep our temper under control to the point where we can transform angry feelings into bodily ailments, such as migraines, tension in our shoulders, aching muscles and raised blood pressure.

If you are experiencing any of these on a regular basis, it is likely that you have moved into the anger stage but are unable to express it. Some ideas for getting anger out into the open are shown later in this section.

Anger, however, is the road to healing and is often the first sign that you are moving out of the first stage of shock and numbness. Depending upon whether you are the leaver or the left, you may be angry about different things and express this in different ways. For example, if you are the leaver and it has taken you a long time to leave the relationship, you may feel angry about time wasted in the past. You may also find yourself feeling angry about things that happened a long time ago. You may even feel angry with yourself.

If you are the person who has been left in the relationship, your anger may be wholly directed at your ex-partner for betraying you and your relationship, for behaviour which is out of character or for leaving you to cope with life alone. Your anger may also be directed at other people within your circle of family and friends, some of whom may be supportive and some of whom may not be. Family separation can cause people to take sides and to empathise with one or other of the parties.

You may feel angry with some of your family and friends and it is important that you are able to identify this so that you do not get into any unnecessary arguments or long-standing feuds at a time when you need your energy for recovery.

Anger is felt and expressed differently by different people.

We are all subject to society's expectations in terms of how we behave, however, and these deeply affect our ability to deal with and express anger in ways that are healthy and healing. Women and men can have very different ways of feeling and expressing anger and it is useful at this point to say a word about this.

ANGER AND WOMEN

Women often find it difficult to express anger. This is often because of the ways in which we are socialised in our society. Although there have been great changes in our attitudes and expectations of women, there is still a widespread assumption that girls and women should be nurturing and caring and kind. These are the qualities that are often associated with being a good mother in our society. This can mean that girls grow up without being able to express anger very well and that by the time they become mothers, they are unable even to feel anger or identify angry feelings.

Many women also find that their angry feelings are transformed into other emotional expression, laughing instead of being angry or crying rather than shouting. Many women who experience depression find that if they are helped to locate and express repressed anger, their depressed mood lifts.

ANGER AND MEN

Men, on the other hand, can find that it is more acceptable to express anger and that, as fathers, they are often expected to be the person who expresses anger towards children in the form of discipline. Men, however, can also find that their anger is unacceptable, particularly expressed within a relationship. With the heightened awareness of domestic abuse, men can feel that it is unacceptable to be angry or to express angry feelings; they might also feel afraid of doing so in case they are assumed to be heading towards being abusive. Some women can also find it difficult when their partner expresses anger towards them and can interpret this as being abusive.

Men's anger and domestic abuse, however, do not go hand in hand. There is a real difference between feeling angry and expressing this in a healthy way and feeling angry and allowing yourself to verbally or physically threaten or attack another person. Anger when expressed healthily is kept within the control of the person who is feeling angry and their actions are always their own responsibility.

PHYSIOLOGY AND ANGER

Anger has a similar action on the body to that of shock in that it releases a cocktail of chemicals into your bloodstream. Adrenalin (epinephrine) and noradrenalin (norepinephrine) are two hormonal chemicals that raise your blood pressure and heighten your physical awareness and strength. It is important, therefore, that anger is expressed whenever it is felt rather than repressed. This is because repression of anger can lead to muscular tension, headaches, sickness and nausea and, in turn, irritability and frustration which simply serve to continue the cycle.

When you have children to care for, who may also be feeling angry, it is useful to find ways of dealing with feelings as they arise. Sometimes it can be useful to share activities designed to reduce anger with children, turning them into games or ways of getting through a difficult day. Whatever you do, however, make sure that your children are expressing their angry feelings and not yours. If you share some of these activities with children it isn't necessary to tell them what you are feeling, or even ask them about their feelings. The main point is that doing something when you are feeling angry is a good way of releasing the anger and reducing its physical and physiological impact on you. Here are a number of tried and tested activities that we and other parents have used to help express and reduce angry feelings. You don't need to use all of them, pick which ones work for you.

Activities to help physically release anger:

- Gardening, especially digging over soil, chopping down trees and sawing wood.

- Walking fast or running, especially in the wind or rain or on a cold day.

- Recycling bottles, smashing them as hard as you can into the bank, but watch your eyes as you do so.

- Smashing crockery on the patio – keep a collection of old pots and plates for this purpose and then use the broken pieces on your garden pots to keep the roots of plants, such as clematis, cool in summer.

- Make your own bread; kneading dough is a really good way of pummelling out your anger.

- Thump cushions, or keep a punchbag in your garage so that you can thump your anger out.

- Go to the seaside and stand on a cliff and scream out your anger.

Sometimes it may not be appropriate to release your anger physically. You may be unable to get outdoors or your children may be too small to share the activities as described above. In this case you can find ways of calming angry feelings until it is possible to work them out physically. Tried and tested ways of calming angry feelings are:

- Having a long, hot soak in the bath.

- Ringing a friend and talking about how you are feeling.

- Listening to music with your eyes closed.

- Drinking tea, especially chamomile tea.

- Knitting or sewing, or some other creative pursuit.

- Tinkering with the car.

- Watching something familiar on DVD, perhaps a sitcom or football.

Sadness and despair

The next stage on the Change Curve is sadness and its companion despair. This stage is more passive than its predecessor and heralds the beginning of emotional acceptance of the change.

If you are the leaver in a relationship, this stage may feel like nostalgia and you may find yourself, at times, inexplicably reminded of your old life and your ex-partner. The stage of sadness and despair may not last long for someone who has left a relationship, especially if the leaving was longed for or planned. If the leaving of the relationship was because of issues, such as domestic abuse, however, or because of other behaviour on the part of your ex-partner, the stage of sadness and despair can be a trigger point for considering returning to the relationship.

If you are the person who has been left in a relationship this stage may come upon you as a feeling of sudden tiredness, weepiness or loneliness. Memories of the past may come back in waves and you may remember all of the things that you loved about your ex-partner and feel unbearable longing for them to come back into your life. As you go through this stage it is important to carry on with all of the things that you have been doing to take care of yourself. This stage, if you are the person who has been left, can leave you feeling bleak and exhausted and uninterested in anything around you.

DEALING WITH SADNESS AND DESPAIR

Many people who pass through this stage talk of feeling as if everything has come to a standstill, as though they have lost the will or energy to keep going. This is the stage where you really begin to accept that the change has happened and that the work to be done is to mourn and grieve the loss of your loved one.

Mourning and grieving the end of a relationship is never easy, particularly in our society. If your loved one has died, there is, at least, a ceremony to say goodbye to them. If your loved one has left you, or if you are the leaver in the relationship, there is very little in the way of public acknowledgement of the mourning and grieving that you need to do in order to move on into a new phase of your life.

Whether you are the leaver or the left in a relationship, it can be useful to mark an acceptance of the end. After all, we spend a great deal of time marking other important events in our lives: marriage, births, birthdays, anniversaries, and so on. Some people use divorce as a way of marking the end of the relationship with the time spent between decree nisi and decree absolute as a sort of holding time during which the mourning and grieving for the relationship are completed. Other people, those perhaps who have not been married, mark the ending in other ways.

How you mark the ending of your relationship is up to you, but it is useful at some point during this stage of sadness and despair to mark for yourself the acceptance that your relationship is finally over and there is no going back. Doing so will help you to move on and will also allow you to separate out the ending of your personal relationship with your ex-partner from the parenting responsibilities that you will continue to share.

So many parents are unable to build new, cooperative relationships after separation, simply because they have not been able to complete properly the mourning and grieving necessary to acknowledge for themselves that the relationship has ended. Too many parents become enmeshed in fights and arguments around arrangements for children, because they have not accepted that the relationship is at an end. Whether you are the leaver or the left, it is important during this stage of sadness that you consciously acknowledge that your relationship is over and that the old way of life has gone. Here are some examples of how parents we have worked with have marked the ending of their relationships.

'I planted a magnolia tree in my garden as a symbol of my new start. In doing so I had to dig up and remove an old cherry tree that we had planted together many years ago. Now, when I look out of the kitchen window, I see something that I planted, something beautiful that is just for

me. Planting that tree marked the end of the old and the start of the new for me.'
Cathy, aged 32 – divorced after being married for 15 years

'My decree nisi came through the post. It was barely six months after she had walked out on me. I had the boys that weekend and I took them to the coast that day and we went paddling. I stood in the water and watched my two wonderful boys jumping over waves and laughing, and I knew then that I wanted them to grow up without the fighting and arguing that had gone on for years. I decided that I would change my life that day even though I felt the most incredible sadness and loneliness; many times after that day I was desperate, but from that day on I stopped looking back and thinking "what if".'
Rob – divorced after being married for ten years

'I went out and got blind drunk on the day that my decree absolute came through and when I woke up I felt so awful that I swore to myself that I would never let him put me through this kind of misery again. I think I was still angry and then sad and then angry again for some time after that, but it was a real ending for me when I woke up that morning.'
Julia – divorced after being married for four years

'We weren't married but I remember the day that I realised that it was over for me. My car had been damaged quite badly in an accident the previous week and I had to collect it from the garage where it was being repaired. As I was walking across the forecourt I saw this lovely red Mini Cooper, a car I had always wanted. I suddenly realised that not only did I want to buy that car, I wanted to buy it for me and me alone. It felt really odd to be thinking solely about myself instead of thinking about how the car would fit into family life. I checked out the space in the back for a child seat for my daughter and then bought it! I went home with it that very day and it made me feel like I was back in control of my life again, despite the sadness and the loneliness. Since then it's not been easy but I know that I moved on that day.'

Dave – separated after seven years

We are not suggesting that marking the ending of the relationship needs to be something as dramatic as buying a new car or getting very drunk. What we do say to parents though, when we are working through the Change Curve, is that while the stage of sadness and despair seems bleak and something most of us would rather not experience, within that stage is the kernel of a new beginning as you start to accept that your life will never be the same again. Finding your own way to mark this for yourself can be a powerful tool for helping yourself to move on to the next stage.

Depression

In our society, depression is a much-used word, and yet in other cultures the word depression does not exist. The literal meaning of depression is 'pressing down upon', and it is this feeling of being pressed down by a weight that best describes this stage of the Change Curve. When you are in this stage you may feel lethargic and very tired. You may also have 'what's the point' thoughts and feel as though everything is either pointless or impossible.

Depression is often a sign that someone has stopped dealing with the external events that caused the change to happen and come to a place where acceptance of the change and its inevitable effects on the future is complete. Not unlike the stage of sadness and despair, depression is a more passive stage of the Change Curve. Depression, though, differs from the sadness stage, primarily because of the lack of, rather than the intensity of, feeling. In this stage it is almost as though there is a complete absence of feeling, a lack of caring for oneself, for other people or even for what has happened to you and your family. The depression stage can last for a week, a month or, when it becomes more complicated, for far longer than that.

Whereas it is not inevitable for either the leaver or the left to go through the depression stage, it is a stage that is likely to be experienced by those who have been left in a relationship. Depression often masks fear: fear of the future, fear of the responsibility to make a new life, fear of failure. When you are the leaver in a relationship you have often encountered the stages of change ahead of your ex-partner, if not in reality, then in your mind. Thinking about leaving a relationship means that you will be considering the future and taking charge of that out of choice, which can mean that there is much less fear around for you.

When you have been left in a relationship you have had choices taken away from you along with the future that you expected to live. Coming to terms with being left in a relationship means that you are forced into a situation where you will have to begin to make choices for yourself and for your children too at some point. Creating a new life for yourself and a new future is going to be a major feature in the time ahead. After the shock and grief of being left, fear of these tasks can be a major reason why many people experience depression.

Depression can be experienced in many different ways and it is important that you are able to determine how severe your depression really is. Many people use the word 'depressed' when they really mean low in mood. We use the word depressed, when we talk about the Change Curve, to describe the stage where people are finally accepting the reality of their situation and are simply too exhausted to do anything else. We do not mean that people are clinically depressed when they are in this stage of the Change Curve, although some people may find their depression is extended beyond a time frame that could be considered to be normal under the circumstances.

Generally speaking, if you have suffered family separation within the previous 18 months and are feeling low in mood, tired and heavy, and afraid to look ahead because it all seems too much for you, we would say that you are in the depression stage. If, however, you have not suffered a major loss, such as family separation, in the previous 18 months, or if the major loss was more than two years previously and you feel low in mood and it all seems too much for you on an ongoing basis, we would suggest that you see a GP and discuss your feelings. It may be that you are experiencing a more complicated reaction to your loss, or, if the depressed feelings come over you without the effect of external issues in your life, such as family separation, that you are experiencing clinical depression for which you may need medication.

DEPRESSION AND MEDICATION

With the rise in popularity of antidepressants, such as Prozac and others in the same family of drugs called SSRIs or selective serotonin reuptake inhibitors, many people may find that their GP is willing to offer prescriptions to help with the process of coming to terms with family separation. At the Centre for Separated Families, we try to make sure that every parent has access to the kind of information that they need to help them decide whether or not they need to take antidepressants.

Taking antidepressants can be useful for some people and can help to alleviate some of the suffering after family separation. If you are low in mood for a long period of time or your feelings are leading towards thoughts of suicide or self-harm, talking to your GP and taking a course of anti-depressants can be the right thing to do. In some cases it may even save your life.

Some people who have experienced the intense suffering that can accompany the depression stage would certainly recommend them. Others, who have suffered equally, might counsel against them saying that they mask the reality of the situation or prevent the completion of the process of psychological change.

Our position at the Centre for Separated Families is that every parent is different and all circumstances are unique to the person who is experiencing them. We take time to discuss the possibilities of medication with parents who find themselves in the depressed stage of the Change Curve and recommend a further discussion with a GP. We also offer counselling to parents throughout their experience of family separation, and where it is clear that someone is in the period of depression that accompanies family change, we might concentrate the focus of this upon helping the client to find out what they are afraid of and dealing with that so they can move on.

What is important to remember is that feeling low in mood after family separation is normal. Providing that the feelings do not last for a very long time and that they do not descend into thoughts of self-harm, you can be sure that eventually the depression will lift and you will start to get a feeling of life moving on for you.

WHEN TO GET EXTRA HELP

You should definitely think about getting extra help if any of the following is true for you:

- Your low mood comes on suddenly and is not related to any external event.

- Your low mood leads to thoughts of self-harm or suicide.

- Your low mood lasts for more than a year.

- Your low mood makes it difficult for you to care for your children or for yourself.

Experimentation

After depression comes a sense of movement and a renewed desire to be out in the world again. This phase may coincide with an anniversary of the separation, or may seem to come out of the blue, as you wake up one morning and just know that things have changed. Sometimes a change of season will bring about a desire to move on. Spring is the season of renewal and many people talk about feeling as though their energy and enthusiasm are returning in the springtime.

THE LEAVER

If you are the leaver in a relationship, this stage of the Change Curve can feel as though it has been very possible from the time that you left to begin your new life. It can also be a stage when you are confused and find yourself feeling sad and low instead of raring to go and try out new things. Arriving at this stage if you are the leaver in a relationship can herald a new sense of relief. At last you have arrived at the place you have been seeking to be for some time and now your expectations are being met.

Free of guilt and sadness, it can be intoxicating to try out new things, new ways of living and new behaviours. This is the stage when, if you left a relationship without moving straight into another one, you may begin to look out for someone new to fall in love with. The only word of caution here is to remember that you are still moving through a period of change, that you are still at risk of slipping back down the Change Curve before you have successfully negotiated the change and that you are still your children's parent wherever your new life is taking you.

THE LEFT

If you are the person who was left in the relationship, this is the stage when you finally experience some relief from the powerful feelings that you have been negotiating for some time now. This stage can feel exciting and challenging and bring with it new opportunities, friends and interests. After a long period of feeling that you do not have any choices in life, suddenly you feel that there are many different choices to be made and many different directions to choose from. The only word of caution that we would offer here is that you too are still at risk of slipping back down the Change Curve and that you continue to be your children's parent, first and foremost.

YOUR NEW LIFE

Further chapters will help you to deal with this stage of the Change Curve in practical terms, helping you to work out how to integrate your new life and the choices that you make with practical issues, such as who looks after the children while you are at evening class, or how you will continue to parent together with your ex-partner, even while you are moving on to pastures new. These are not easy things to deal with, but they are the very things that require your attention just as you feel that you have come through the worst.

Being aware of where you are in the Change Curve and being aware that your ex-partner is likely to be in a very different place to you can help you to decide on the best approach to starting to talk about how you are going to co-parent in the future. Recovery from your family separation is essential if you are going to build a more businesslike relationship with your ex-partner. But recovery, when you still have a long parenting journey ahead of you, does not mean throwing off the old without a second thought. As a separated parent, it is an irony that just as you start to feel that you are ready for your new life, you are tasked with finding a way of reconnecting with the old, albeit in a new and more businesslike way.

Confidence returns and integration

The final stages of the Change Curve bring a renewed confidence in yourself and your ability to cope with life. If you are the leaver in a relationship, this stage can appear to have arrived before it actually has, particularly if you moved straight into a new relationship after your old one ended. This stage can often feel like the first stage of a new relationship as you feel good about yourself again and confident in your life choices.

A word of caution here if you are the leaver in a relationship and you feel like this just after you have left your old relationship behind. It is important to remember that whether you chose the ending of the relationship or not, certain psychological changes must take place before you have fully integrated the change in your life.

If it is less than six months since you left your last relationship and if you moved straight into a new one either before or immediately after your old one ended, what you are feeling is unlikely to be the final stage of the Change Curve. What you are more likely to be feeling is the intoxication of new love and all of the feelings of liberation that come with being free to be involved in that.

Remember, though, that all relationships go through certain phases too and that even if you are feeling on top of the world now, if you are new to the relationship and your old one finished less than six months ago, you are very likely, at some point soon, to experience a change in those feelings. Sooner or later, whether you are the leaver or the left, you will have to deal with the emotional impact of ending your relationship. None of us can escape it although few of us recognise it.

If you are the leaver in a relationship, whether you moved into a new one or not and it is two years or more since your old relationship ended and you are feeling more confident again, you are likely to be through to the other side of the Change Curve. This means that you have successfully negotiated the tasks required to assimilate change fully.

If you were the person who was left in a relationship and you are feeling more confident and find yourself enjoying new and old interests again, it is likely that you are approaching the ending of your travel through the Change Curve. When you have fully assimilated the change of family separation after being left in a relationship, you may feel stronger, wiser and calmer. You can congratulate yourself at this point, for having faced some very big feelings and some terrifying experiences. You might even find yourself helping others through the worst of it as you look back over the progress you have made.

Being left in a relationship can make you feel a
you are powerless and can force you to question ev
about yourself, so surviving this is a real achieveme
you are ready to move on into your new life and, at tl
time, you have successfully achieved separation fror
ex-partner. This is the point at which cooperative par
can work well for all concerned.

All in its own time

It is important at this stage to highlight the fact that whe
we all progress through the Change Curve after import
life-changing events, we do not all progress through it at
same pace. It is rare for us to find that our ex-partners
progressing through change at the same rate; in fact, we
not know of even one ex-couple who have done so. Th
reality is that the Change Curve is merely a road map for u
to use individually, a way of helping us to determine where
we are psychologically and emotionally and where we might
be heading.

At the Centre for Separated Families we work with ex-
couples individually using the Change Curve. Our purpose is
to help parents to identify where they are on the curve and
to identify where they think their ex-partner may be. By
doing this we aim to help a parent to understand that their
experience is not the same as their children's other parent. By
doing this we aim to help parents to understand more fully
what is happening to each of them and why. We do this
precisely at the time when most people who are separating
would be concentrating upon moving away emotionally
from their ex-partner.

We do this because we know that parents who are separating have to keep on being mum and dad to their children
and that the early days and weeks of family separation are

crucial to the long-term relationships between mothers and fathers and their children. What we are doing when we work with ex-partners in this way is trying to help each to deal with the emotional and psychological impact of family separation in a conscious way so that they can avoid getting stuck in patterns of conflict that often arise from one or both getting stuck in one of the stages of the Change Curve.

Conclusion

We are ending this chapter by offering you a number of our own survival strategies for the early days after family separation. We know how hard it is to cope with day-to-day living and caring for children when your family life has erupted into emotional and physical chaos.

Survival strategies in the early stages

Some of these strategies are straight from our own lives; others have been collected from the parents we have worked with over the years. Try the one that sounds right for you and if it works, fine, use it as much as you need to. If not, try another and another until you find one that does work for you. The main thing to keep in mind is that you are not on your own in this, other people have gone through this kind of upheaval and have survived. Many of them have also thrived and their children have too.

Family separation is a painful and disorientating experience but, with time and a lot of self-care, you and your children, and in a different way your ex-partner too, can continue to be a family, albeit a separated family.

SURVIVING THE FIRST DAYS

1. If you cannot face working because you are too distressed, visit your GP and explain what has happened and ask for some time off work.

2. Explain to your boss what has happened and reassure him or her that you need to take time to settle yourself and then you will return to work as normal.

3. Establish a new routine for yourself and stick to it.

4. Get up at the same time every morning and eat break-fast without fail.

5. Find two or more people in whom you can confide. Instead of ringing them or calling round to see them and pouring out all of your feelings, ask them for permission to talk to them on a regular basis about how you feel and promise that you will limit this to an hour at a time. This ensures that you get regular time to talk about what is happening to you but you won't over-burden your friends and end up isolated.

6. Limit your alcohol intake; especially do not drink alone at night.

7. Limit your cigarette intake; the nicotine will make the physical impact on your body much worse.

8. Limit your tea and coffee intake; these, too, make the physical impact worse.

9. Get family members in to help with caring for your

children but do make sure that you also spend as much quiet time with your children as you can.

10. Structure your days so that you can get out of the house for at least a couple of hours every day. If you have small children, take them to the park every morning or every afternoon.

SURVIVING LONGER TERM

Having survived the first days after separation, the following suggestions may help you to cope longer term:

1. Find a good counsellor – the address for finding a counsellor is in Resources, at the end of the book.

2. Make a meal every day and sit at the table to eat it.

3. Keep building new routines – find a new café to meet friends in.

4. Go to a new pub with a friend.

5. Start a new hobby – one that you can share with other people on a weekly basis.

6. Write a diary of how you are feeling.

7. Write a list of the books you would like to read when you are ready.

8. Play football with your mates every week.

9. Join the local library and take the children there once a week.

10. Find something new that you can do with your children on a regular basis – ideas for this are endless. Here are a few that we tried: kayaking, tae kwon do, karate, sailing remote-control boats in the river, walking around the village before bedtime every night (including dark nights and when it was raining!), horseriding and cinema trips to see old films.

Not everything has to cost money, especially when children are younger it is possible to do something new on a daily basis with them. The point of doing something new every day is to set up a period of time when your children know that they will have your undivided attention. This helps you to cope with the day, because it means that outside of this time you can work towards helping your children to entertain themselves, meaning that you can get jobs done or simply sit and have a cup of tea if things are too overwhelming for you, or if you are in the angry or sad stages of recovery. It also means that your children have a clear routine, including regular and predictable access to your undivided attention, which is vital for their reassurance and ability to come to terms with the family change.

We found that it was often during these daily one- or two-hour activity times that our children would talk about what was happening in the family and how they felt about it. This meant that we were able to provide reassurance on a daily basis without needing to interrogate or question our children.

We tried decoupage (sticking pictures onto pieces of furniture to make them brightly coloured). You can buy decoupage kits but we made our own from magazines and children's comics. We also tried clay modelling, making picture frames out of papier-mâché, building the highest tower out of Lego, painting, drawing, writing stories.

We found that in doing these activities with our children, we were also helping ourselves enormously because in the doing of them, we were able to forget for a while some of the feelings that we were having to deal with.

SURVIVING THE DAYS WHEN YOU THINK YOU CANNOT GO ON

Sometimes it can all just feel impossible. If this is one of those days then do not try to force yourself to do anything, just give in. If you are alone, get a blanket and curl up under it on the sofa and watch TV; in our experience, when you are in this state, any old rubbish will do.

If you have your children with you then get them to curl up under the blanket with you and read stories for a while, set up camp in your living room and pretend you are all on an island. Get the children to bring in their favourite toys and make a tray of sandwiches and drinks with little plates of snacks and treats to get you through the day.

If it is a hot summer day, set up camp outside in the garden or open all of the windows if you don't have a garden so that you can let fresh air in and then set up camp in your living room.

If it is one of those days that you think you just cannot survive, call a friend and talk, call a family member and talk, call the Samaritans and talk, call the Centre for Separated Families and talk, or read through some of the personal stories in this book. Whatever you do, you must survive, for your children and for yourself. Believe us, this too will pass and it's worth it in the long run.

Personal Story
Phil – married for seven years – with two children aged six and four

I got married when I was 21, which was too young really I suppose, although it didn't feel like that at the time. I had been with Nikki since I was 17 and we just felt that it was the right thing to do. I was working as an apprentice and she was working for an insurance firm, and we wanted to buy a house and live together so getting married seemed like the natural thing to do.

We had a really big wedding. It was a bit of a nightmare to get organised although I wasn't really all that involved in that side of things. I remember thinking it was a right old palaver and that we should just go off to Barbados and get married on our own.

Anyway we bought our dream house – well, it was our dream house, then, I suppose – a new house on a brand-new estate. We thought we had gone up in the world a bit and spent a good deal of time during the first year playing house and having our friends round for meals. Nikki got pregnant pretty quickly after we got married although it was a bit of a shock to me as she hadn't told me that she was coming off the pill. She was happy though and so I couldn't really say anything. Quite soon after we had our first baby though she wanted another one and I didn't think it was good idea.

We didn't have much money and Nikki had stopped working which meant that we had even less, and I was worried all the time that we wouldn't be able to manage. Anyway, shortly after our first had her second birthday, our second baby was born, and I was really happy that year I remember. It felt as though our family was complete and that we could look forward to many years together sharing the kids growing up. The next four years went by happily it seemed to me, and then in the September our youngest child went to school and Nikki went back to work part-time at the big insurance company in town.

At first I didn't notice that anything had changed. Nikki would go off to work after dropping the kids at school and would be home in time to pick them up. I would come in at 6.30 p.m. and we would all eat our tea together and then I would sort out the kids' clothes for the next day and read them a story before bedtime while Nikki washed up and had a cup of tea watching one of the soap operas. It was a quiet routine and one that I was very happy with. We had started to feel a bit more financially secure and we were even talking about going abroad for a holiday that year, which felt really exciting.

One night, when I got in from work, Nikki was quite short with me. She said I would have to make tea as she hadn't got time as she was going out. I was quite taken aback at this as she would usually let me know ahead of time if she was planning to go out at night so that I could come home earlier and get the tea on for the kids. I asked her if everything was OK and she said yes and went off, I thought, to see one of her friends. I didn't think any more about it really.

The next thing was she came home and said that she was going away for the weekend on a training course with work. Again I didn't think anything about it. She had been away before with work so I had no reason to think that there was anything untoward going on with this weekend away.

Unfortunately for Nikki and, I suppose, fortunately for

me, that weekend I bumped into one of her workmates from the same section. When I asked why she hadn't gone on the training course too, the look on her face told me everything I needed to know. There was no training course and Nikki had lied to me. Worse than that she was off somewhere with someone and I had no idea where she was. She didn't have a mobile and so I had to wait until she rang later on that evening to check on the kids to find out where she was and who she was with.

The days after that were dreadful. I was a complete wreck and didn't know what to do with myself. It turned out that Nikki had been seeing this bloke for several months and that she had been planning to leave me even if I hadn't found out about it that weekend. I was so shocked and so hurt. I couldn't speak for several days and I know that the children were frightened by that.

When Nikki got back we tried to sit and talk but I was just too upset and she seemed to have changed beyond recognition. I realise now that my finding out was a relief to her because it meant that she didn't need to tell me herself. She just seemed to me to be cold and indifferent and I couldn't believe that she could be so cruel.

We fought a lot in those first two weeks after I found out. She wanted to leave immediately and take the children with her to live with this man but I just refused to let her do that. I was determined that she was not going to take the children to live with a stranger and that they would stay with me in their own home. Nikki, quite understandably, did not want to leave without the children, and so there were a couple of weeks when we really fought each other, taking out all of the hurt and pain on each other, each of us trying to win the fight to have our children with us. I am sure that we did some real damage

41

to our children during that time. The fights must have been terrifying for them, they were terrifying for me and for Nikki too, I suppose.

The difficulty when your children's other parent wants to leave and take the children too is that they are not only taking away their love for you and yours for them, they are taking away the love you share for your children, and not only that but your children too. The thought of a stranger reading stories to my children at night almost killed me. I knew that I was going to do everything I possibly could to keep my children living in their own home, with me. The fights went on and on.

Eventually we were exhausted, and Nikki said that she was going to move out anyway and that she would have the children to live with her for part of the week if I would agree to it. I still wouldn't agree though, I didn't want my children to live with another man and their mother; I knew that if they did, it would be too easy for them to start to see that as being their real family and me as being the outsider.

So many people seemed to think I was in the wrong for putting up a fight to keep my children with me. I was just obsessed with it. At the same time though I was just trying to survive and to provide some semblance of normality for my children, some connection to their ordered life in the past. I wanted them to go to bed in their own bedrooms and to come home from school in the same way.

After Nikki moved out, I asked my boss if I could work part-time for a while and I was lucky as he said yes. Not many men get the chance to do that these days; most jobs for men are full-time. I worked out that I could pay the mortgage on my part-time wage and still be able to

eat and pay the bills. I wanted Nikki to give me something every week to help towards things like clothes for
the kids but she wouldn't. She said that she would spend
the money she wanted to spend on them when they were
with her and that I would just have to manage. So I did
manage, but it was a very poor existence for me – and the
kids, I suppose – for a while.

At first I felt bloody miserable every time I woke up. I
couldn't sleep properly for months, but I made sure that I
went to bed at the same time every night and got up at
7.30 a.m. to get the kids up and off to school. If I wasn't
working, I would come home and do some housework,
get the kids' clothes washed and the washing-up done.
After that, in the first year, I would just sit down and
watch the news at 1.00 p.m. and then fall asleep on the
settee until it was time to go and collect the kids from
school.

I didn't go out at all for the first six months. I just
couldn't face seeing anyone. My mum would come down
on Sunday morning and would help me to make a good
Sunday roast. Then she would drop the kids off with
Nikki and they would stay there until I picked them up at
7.00 p.m. What really saved me I suppose, during those
first months, was playing football on a Sunday afternoon.
When I felt at my worst, I would get my kit on and get
out into the freezing weather and play as hard as I could.
The lads there were really good to me. They never said
much to me directly but I could tell that they were
rooting for me. After we finished a game we would go to
the pub for a pint for a couple of hours. It was during
those Sunday afternoons that I would recharge and feel
myself getting together again.

After the first year things got a bit better. Nikki left the bloke she had moved in with and got her own flat. This meant that the kids could stay with their mum and that there were no worries on my part about them being around someone who was a stranger. Things felt different somehow and the kids enjoyed seeing their mum so much that I felt that I should do something to make things easier for everyone. I rang Nikki one day and asked her to meet me to talk about things. We met up in a café and whereas I can't say that the meeting was easy, we did end up agreeing to try to arrange things so that the kids could stay with her for a couple of nights every week.

Anyway, we did get into this routine where she would pick them up on a Monday from school and have them until Thursday when my mum picked them up from school. I was then able to go back to work full-time which wasn't easy, particularly as I had to fit in all the house-work and shopping and after-school activities too, but it meant we had quite a bit more money. Finally I was able to take them abroad. We went to France for two weeks camping and had a whale of a time. Nikki wasn't very happy about that because she couldn't afford to take them on holiday but there wasn't much I could do about it.

The kids are 13 and 11 now and they live with me for half of the week and Nikki for the other half. We take it in turns to have them at weekends and try to make arrangements for Christmas so that the kids are not having to interrupt their days and pack all their things up to move. Eventually I would like them to be able to decide for themselves who they are with and when.

I feel as if I have managed the change quite well, I suppose. I was a complete wreck at first and could hardly speak for the first few days after I found out that Nikki had been having an affair. I went into shock I think, and the only thing that got me through the days was the thought of keeping my children in their own home with me.

I did some things that I would recommend to other people going through the same thing. I never ever talked about the situation in front of the children and I never said anything horrible or bad about Nikki in front of the kids. If she hadn't gone off with another bloke I think I would have been more relaxed about them being with her, but I am glad that I didn't let them go with her because in the end they split up anyway. I am glad my children didn't have to go through that experience again so shortly after we had separated.

It took about two and a half years for me to feel that I was starting again and that I was over the ending of my relationship with Nikki. By that time Nikki had been to see someone at the Centre for Separated Families because she wanted to change the arrangements and didn't know how to. They helped us to talk about things together and offered me some time to talk to someone every week, a bit like counselling I suppose. These sessions really helped me to get things into perspective and I started to feel more confident about myself and about the way in which I was coping. That meant that I didn't feel so defensive around Nikki all the time, and I was able to agree to changing the arrangements for the children quite easily.

I haven't met anyone else yet, but this year I have felt that I might be ready to do so. If I do meet someone I will take it very slowly and not introduce them to the kids until I know for sure that it is going to be long-lasting. Now that I have more spare time I can see friends easily without it interrupting my life with the kids. I am happy that I have got to this place. It's been hard work and I have been incredibly sad at times, so much so that I know I will never be the same. But life is good again – different, but good. Best of all I am still a dad to my kids and I know now that nothing can change that.

Chapter 2

Your Relationship with Your Ex-Partner

THE ENDING OF a relationship, particularly one that has involved being parents to children, is rarely an easy thing to negotiate. Most people will experience a complicated range of emotions and find that these will be dominant at different times and to different depths.

Consider your own feelings. Have you felt pain? Maybe it was you who decided to leave the relationship and ending things has left you with a sense of relief. Perhaps it was you who was left but still you have felt a sense of relief. Maybe you have felt angry, either about the cause of the separation or the injustice that you have felt from being left. It is very common to feel just plain sad; sad about the ending of the relationship, about the hopes that were never fulfilled or about the tainting of some of your memories of happier times.

In Chapter 1, we looked at how these emotions are likely to affect you. However, it is also crucial that we can understand the ways in which these will affect your ongoing relationship with your ex-partner. Emotions must be dealt with if you are to reduce conflict and build a post-separation parenting relationship in which children can feel secure and happy.

Even where the decision to separate has been a mutual one, it is rare that parents will be able to slip easily into a post-separation relationship that is uncomplicated and free from conflict. Indeed, conflict, in a strange way, is one of the devices that couples use in order to hang on to a relationship, even though it has ended – either for one or both parties.

While you have been together you will, almost certainly, have shared many intimate experiences, none greater than parenting together. If you are both the biological parents of your children, then it is likely that you will have shared the hope of the pregnancy, the joy of birth, the anxiety of being responsible for the little life that you have created between you, the pleasure of the first steps and first words, and the fear of illness.

If your relationship was long-lasting, you may also have watched your children make their first forays into the world around them: their first day at school, their first school play or sports day.

These are things that the pair of you will have experienced in a way that no one else will have. They are private and intimate and are likely to run through your relationship like a golden thread. Then, one day, the thread is cut and you each become separate curators of those precious memories. You must each face the awful prospect of having to recall them on your own – each time a reminder of the ending of your relationship, accompanied with feelings of loss, failure and a sense of those special moments having been tarnished by the ending of your relationship.

Is there any wonder, then, that couples who separate, regardless of whether they are the leaver or the left, struggle to let go of the relationship fully? Or that they will use any device possible that will maintain a connection between those intimate times that you both shared and the separate individuals that you have become?

The tasks of separation

Separation is not an easy business. It's not simply a question of deciding not to live together. It requires a high degree of emotional and psychological disentanglement. It requires you to see yourself as a single person again or, at least, a person who is no longer in a relationship with the other parent.

Regardless of how sad, happy, relieved, bitter, humiliated, elated, justified, hurt, guilty, angry, surprised, unsurprised or downright bloody furious you are, there is, nevertheless, a process that you will need to go through in order to come out the other side having dealt properly with your emotional and psychological reactions.

And you need to do this not just to allow yourself to move forward but to enable you to provide the stability that your children require and to help you minimise the potential for conflict with the other parent. If you are unable to acknowledge and deal with how you feel then you are unlikely to be able to help your children deal with what they feel, and the potential for conflict with the other parent is never going to be far away.

Separating fully from your ex-partner is about reclaiming yourself as an individual human being. It's about separating yourself out from the old relationship and seeing yourself as 'I' rather than 'we'. This will help you to re-establish the things that you are personally capable of, the things that you may need help with and to see how you will be able to adapt these to your new parenting relationship.

There are three main tasks of separation that must be completed before you are ready to move on.

Physical separation

You have decided that your relationship has ended, and with that comes a physical separation. You may still be living in the same house but no longer sharing a bed. You may have already begun to live in different homes. Physical separation can be easy if you were the person who instigated the separation but very difficult if you were taken by surprise or the separation is very much against your wishes.

Physical separation, particularly if you were together for a long time or spent a great deal of your time together, can be very painful. Physically moving apart, however, is only the beginning of a process that can, for some people, take a long time, sometimes as long as two years or more. The tasks of separation run alongside the Change Curve processes which were outlined in Chapter 1 and can be thought of as ways of marking your progress through the change in your family life. Remember that your children also have tasks of separation to complete too and that they will require your help to complete these and integrate the change.

Physical separation can happen overnight when one partner has already decided that the relationship has ended, or it can take several weeks and sometimes months to complete fully. It is not uncommon for separating couples to find themselves back together in the same bed, one night, recalling memories of times past and finding reassurance from old familiar feelings. This can be just a one-off occurrence, or it can happen several times. If this is a situation that you find yourself in try not to punish yourself if you feel bad about it and, if you feel good about it, try to keep in mind that it may not herald the rekindling of your ex-partner's feelings.

Some people find that separation is an extremely difficult and painful process, and whereas they are yearning for their new life, their fear and anxiety about being out there on their own can mean that they come back for reassurance over and over before they finally leave. If you are in a situation where your ex-partner keeps instigating sex or emotional closeness only to disappear the next day, be very careful, particularly when your children are in the house and wake up to find mummy and daddy back in their old bed. Children may think that this signifies that things are back to normal when, actually, the truth is that the two of you ended up having sex 'for old times' sake'.

The task of physical separation is complete when you have established separate lives and have begun to build new routines and a new way of life. When you are regularly seeing your ex-partner during the times that children are moving between you and this doesn't lead to a cup of tea, glass of wine and more, you can be sure that you have completed the first task of separation.

The next task is more complicated than the first and involves separating yourselves emotionally. This may seem easy but, as we will go on to describe, the ways in which we hang on to our emotional involvement with ex-partners are not always easy to spot.

Emotional separation

There is such an overwhelming rush of emotion surrounding family separation that it is surprising that we can still carry out ordinary everyday tasks. People describe waves of anger, of feeling flooded with sadness and despair and as if they have been hit by a steamroller. Our best advice is that if you are experiencing high levels of emotion in the weeks after family separation, don't try to remain stoic; don't try to keep a stiff upper lip. Let your feelings of sadness and despair be known to your family and friends.

Failure to mourn the ending of your relationship can result in a preoccupation with your ex-partner that will, in turn, prevent either of you from moving on. In fact, failure to grieve – to give vent fully to those feelings of sadness – is one of the ways in which we continue to involve ourselves in our ex-partner's life. If we do not grieve we can remain enmeshed with them, at least on an emotional level, at least in our own mind.

Remaining enmeshed emotionally with your ex-partner can be displayed in many different ways, from pretending that you can still be friends and ringing them up for a chat every other day, to screaming and shouting in fury at them whenever you happen to meet. Paradoxically, those couples with the highest levels of conflict after family separation are those who remain the most emotionally enmeshed. As we have said, conflict is one of the devices that couples use to prolong their emotional connection.

If you find that you are regularly infuriated about things that your ex-partner says or does, or if you find that you cannot separate out your children's relationship with their other parent from your relationship with your ex-partner, you are still likely to be emotionally connected. Emotional separation in these circumstances is crucial if you are going to build a cooperative parenting relationship because, if you cannot separate emotionally, you are in danger of using your children as tools to keep your connection to your ex-partner.

You will know that you are on the way to emotional separation when you are able to talk to your ex-partner without feeling anxious, angry or frustrated. Getting to the point where you are able to identify which feelings are a hangover from the separation and which are about genuine current concerns is not easy, however, so here are a few pointers to help you.

- When you feel yourself getting angry with your ex-partner, stop and think about what is really going on. Are you angry because of what has happened to your relationship or because of the way that they are currently behaving?

- You may, for example, feel that you are angry because your ex-partner has not brought the children home on time again. Consider whether what you are really experiencing is a loss of control over your ex-partner's behaviour.

- You may feel upset because your ex-partner has just bought a new car. You may believe that this means that she isn't looking after the children properly as she is spending money that she hasn't got. However, in reality, your feelings may have arisen because you are jealous that your ex-partner has a new car while you are still driving around in a battered old heap of junk.

- You might become angry that your children are not being looked after properly when they are with your ex-partner because he doesn't put them to bed on time. Is it really that you are feeling this way because you don't want your children to spend time with their father when you wish they were with you?

Many scenarios arise between two people who are struggling to separate emotionally, and parents often find themselves torn apart by emotions that appear to suggest that they have an intense dislike for each other, whereas, in reality, they mean that they are still emotionally dependent or connected. What we find in our work with separated parents is that those who are involved in the most highly conflicted situations around their children are those who are still having a relationship, albeit a negative one.

For some people who are unable to let go, conflict becomes a means to hang on to a relationship; after all, if you can still get under the other person's skin you must still matter to them at some level.

If you feel that you and your ex-partner are still emotionally enmeshed but are ready to begin the process of separating, learning new ways of communicating can be a good place to start. Breaking old patterns and habits and finding a way of ending difficult scenes are all part of emotional separation (there are some ideas about communication later in this chapter). You will know that you are moving on when you start to feel less interested in what your ex-partner is doing or saying and more interested in the new things in your own life.

Psychological separation

The final task of separation is psychological, which means that you are able to *experience* yourself as separate from your ex-partner. Your psychology is the way that you think about yourself in relation to the world around you and, in terms of your relationship with your ex-partner, psychological separation occurs when you are able to think about yourself as an individual person, separate from your ex-partner and separate from your previous family relationship.

Psychological separation can also mean that you are able to think about your children and their relationship with their other parent and how you are no longer involved in this.

Psychological separation denotes a real shift in thinking, from the past to the future, and is sometimes signalled by a reduction in conflict in your relationship with your ex-partner. If you are more able to deal with your ex-partner in a businesslike manner and have started to think about them as your children's other parent rather than your ex-partner, you are likely to have completed the tasks of separation.

The key things to keep in mind about the tasks of separation are that they are stages on the way to recovering a sense of self and an ability to build a cooperative relationship with your children's other parent.

Separation is not a one-step process but a series of tasks to be completed but, along the way, there are different tools that you can use to speed your progress. Remember that emotional separation takes some time and can be the most difficult task to complete. Dealing with conflict is the major area to resolve if you are going to complete your emotional separation, and this is what we will deal with next.

Conflict

It is a fact that it is not divorce or separation, in themselves, which cause the greatest amount of harm to children, it is the levels of conflict that they experience between their parents.

It is quite possible for children to adapt to, and thrive in, a separated family, but this won't happen by magic, and it is the job of the adults to make this possible, not the children.

Children living in intact families who are exposed to high levels of parental conflict will display the symptoms of the damage that this causes to them. They are more likely to exhibit aggressive and defiant behaviour, suffer from anxiety and depression and carry the burden of lower self-esteem. If you and the other parent fail to develop strategies to minimise conflict then your children will suffer.

If there were high levels of conflict before your family separated – and perhaps high levels of conflict were the cause of your separation – you may already recognise some of these symptoms in your children. These may become worse as a result of the separation or, if high levels of conflict or violence were present in the relationship, the separation may bring relief.

The point is that, regardless of the circumstances of your previous family relationship, you are now embarking on the creation of a new parenting relationship that can be different and possibly better than the one you had when you shared the same house and the same bed. Regardless of what you felt or feel about the other parent or the ending of the relationship, you both have the power to create a new parenting relationship in which your children will feel safe and be able to prosper.

It is important that you don't despair about becoming a 'single parent'. Guilt is an equally unhelpful emotion, and revenge may make you feel better but it will harm your children. In a strange way, understanding that you have both the power and the responsibility to have a positive impact on your children's lives can be very important in helping you to come to terms with the ending of your relationship with the other parent. Taking control of the situation and building for the future can make you feel less helpless. It can be tough and, at times, painful but the rewards come through your children's ongoing – or even new – sense of security and happiness.

Separating parents do not need to become great friends again, neither do they need to forgive or forget. But they can and do need to build a new parenting relationship that acknowledges that, whatever they feel about the other parent, their children still see them as just 'mum' or 'dad'.

The negative impact of conflict

It may seem to be stating the obvious to suggest that conflict is not a good environment in which to move forward after a separation. Clearly, conflict brings with it high levels of stress and, for most people, unhappiness.

Conflict is highly likely to be present around the ending of a relationship, regardless of whether those that are separating have children, or not. Dealing with the needs of children and worrying about your future with them and all the attendant concerns will make you feel unsafe and is likely to be an added cause of conflict between the two of you.

As we have seen, though, this conflict may provide a glimmer of reassurance between you and the other parent of your children because, as long as there is conflict, there is a link between your old lives together and your new lives apart.

In parenting terms, this behaviour has a dual impact. First, your children, regardless of how hard you try to protect them from it, will undoubtedly witness the conflict or the effects of conflict. This leaves them feeling frightened and insecure and brings with it a whole range of other emotions that we will explore in Chapter 3.

The second negative impact that conflict has on the chances of moving forward to a new, cooperative post-separation parenting relationship is that it imprisons you both in the past. It allows you the comfort of not having to deal with the reality of your new situation and prevents you from achieving a different way of continuing to parent together, apart.

The task that you and your former partner have is to stop seeing each other as the 'ex' and to focus on seeing each other as your child's or children's parents. Not convinced? Think of it from your children's perspective. To them, you are just mum and dad, the two most significant adults in their lives – and that doesn't end simply because your adult loving relationship is at an end.

Why conflict is common

'When I found out that he had been having an affair, I just wanted him out of my life and away from my children.'
Wendy – mother of David aged ten and Bryan aged eight.

Relationships end in different ways. Sometimes, both people in the relationship will have known that the end was more or less inevitable for months or even years. At other times, the ending will come to either you or your partner completely out of the blue and as a great shock. If the ending has come to either one of you as a shock, then it is highly likely that this is going to be a source of ongoing conflict.

One of the most common reasons for a seemingly sudden split is that one of the partners has been having a sexual relationship outside the partnership. The discovery of this, either accidentally or because the fact is announced as a prelude to leaving, can be hugely distressing to the other partner.

Being told by your partner – a person in whom you placed trust – that they have been having a relationship with another person will almost certainly leave you feeling hurt, humiliated, angry, mistrustful and, quite possibly, vengeful.

These same emotions are likely to be experienced with any major revelation. For example, lies over money matters or an announcement about sexual orientation. Whatever the announcement, whatever the shock, whatever the 'betrayal', the range of emotions that are outlined above are likely to lead to immediate conflict and provide a difficult background to building your new, post-separation parenting relationship.

It may well be that you will never be able to forgive your former partner for the 'wrong' that they have done you. Building a new, post-separation parenting relationship doesn't require you to do so. However, it will not be possible for you to achieve this unless you are able to separate your experience of the hurt that you have suffered from your children's need for both of you to continue to be good parents.

A detailed exploration of recognising and dealing with your feelings around the separation can be found in Chapter 1. It is important that you try to come to some understanding about what is happening to both yourself and your former partner in order to be equipped to move on.

Identifying your own feelings

If you had the 'wrong' done to you, then you need to identify and deal with your feelings. If you were the person who perpetrated the 'wrong', then you need to understand the feelings that the other parent may be experiencing and also deal with your own emotions, such as guilt and, possibly, regret.

However, this task is not an end in itself nor is it a way to establish a hierarchy of hurt or wrongs done. It is no good simply establishing what has happened and what it has meant to you both.

In the context of post-separation parenting, it needs to be a tool to enable you to separate out what you feel about what you have done to each other in the past in order that you can begin to focus on what you will both do for your child or children in the future.

Whether your separation has come to you as a shock or whether you have been waiting for it for some time, whether you think that you have caused it or been a victim of it, you are almost certainly going to run up against some very practical issues very quickly as a result of the separation, and, unless you both learn to deal with them, you will find yourselves in conflict.

What do you fight about?

In our experience there are four major issues that cause conflict between separated parents who are trying to build a new parenting relationship, and all of these need to be thought about and addressed by both parents. The four major issues are:

- Money

- Parenting time

- Decision making

- Parenting values

We will revisit these issues in Chapter 6 where we discuss the different ways that you might make arrangements for care of the children between the two of you. Here, though, we are looking at how each of these issues contributes to conflict and what you might do to reduce this.

Money

A leading contender for the number-one spot in the list of issues for conflict is money.

Issues around money may have been a problem while you were together. You and your partner may have had different priorities when it came to spending money – you may have felt that holidays were important, your partner may have felt that saving for the future was more important. You may have had different ideas about who had access to the money and how it was divided.

Money may have been the major cause of your separation; for example, your former partner may have had gambling debts. But even if your financial arrangements were not a source of conflict before you separated, they are likely to become so after separation.

The main reason for this is the instability of your new situation and the fact that the costs of living apart will be higher than those of living together. In addition, all of those little niggles around money that were largely hidden when you lived together will come sharply into focus when you separate. Does your former partner really need to buy all those new clothes? Do they really need to be going out with their friends when the children need new coats?

You will also need to work out how you are going to share any assets that you may have and divide any income. This will be complicated by the fact that, as parents, you need to consider the needs of your children as well as those of yourselves. Indeed, one of the main sources of conflict is around the access to and payment of support for children.

The settling of financial disputes is also an area into which separating parents can bring in third parties, such as Family Court judges, to adjudicate. It, therefore, becomes tempting to use issues around money as a way to assert the rightness or wrongness of your separation or to use them to exact retribution for the hurt you feel that you have suffered.

Deal with money but be careful not to let it dominate. We see so many cases where parents who have separated will use the division of money and other resources as either a measure of how wronged they were – that is, the more you can get out of the other parent the clearer it is that they were the 'baddy' – or as a way to exact retribution on the other parent.

The reason that you need to deal with money is so that you and your children can feel financially secure. Your children should not experience financial insecurity or poverty in their relationships with *either* parent, and so it is important that you don't inadvertently punish your children because you feel a need to punish your former partner.

Parenting time

One of the other considerations that is likely to be a cause of conflict is the time you each spend with your children.

Our work with separated families has shown us, over and over again, that this not only causes conflict because of parents' different expectations but can increase it because it is used as a bargaining chip or as a stick with which to beat the other parent.

It is important, at this point, to look at how gendered assumptions about what the 'proper' roles for mothers and fathers are impacts on the situation you are likely to find yourselves in when you separate.

Whether we like it or not, whether we subscribe to it or not, the prevailing custom in most cultures – and that includes most of those found in the United Kingdom, North America, Australia, New Zealand and South Africa – sees the predominant role for women as that of carer and that of men as provider. (This is explored more fully in Chapter 6.) However, it is important that we look at this in the context of your post-separation relationship and your expectations about your continued role as a parent.

Since the 1960s, we have experienced fairly profound changes in gender politics. Women have demanded the right to enter the workplace as the equals of men. Access to education and training has meant that girls have much greater opportunities to take up more challenging occupations than, certainly, their grandmothers might have expected. And women are now, at least, better represented in other areas of public life, whether they are in politics or the media.

Many men, at least partially, have taken up the feminist challenge to take a greater role in the home. Men are now far more likely to be expected to take an interest in pregnancy, the birth of children and children's development. Indeed, some families arrange themselves so that it is the father who does most of the hands-on caring while the mother works outside the home in paid employment. It is also true that many families arrange their affairs on more traditional lines of mother at home and father at work.

What is important to recognise, however, is that regardless of how you organised things before your separation, you are likely to have this interrupted not only by your separation but also by the gender assumptions that are at play in and around the family justice system.

The fact is that you will no longer be treated as equal parents. For example, in the United Kingdom currently, one of you will be accorded the status of 'parent with care' and the other will have to make do with 'non-resident parent' (still commonly, and wrongly, referred to as 'absent parent'). For some people, this may not cause a problem in itself as it may, largely, reflect your pre-separation arrangements. But, where it does not, it is likely to be a source of real anguish and dispute between you and your former partner.

Let's look at a couple of case studies.

Daniel and Cathy

They have one son called Gareth who is three and a half years old. Cathy has been recognised as the parent with care and as such feels that while she doesn't want Daniel to stop seeing their son, she wants to develop her life with her new partner Paul. She intends this relationship to be lasting and sees Paul as the major father figure in Gareth's life. After all, Gareth is still a toddler and so long as he is with his mum, he will also be with Paul.

Daniel is angry that Cathy has left him for a new relationship with Paul and feels both hurt and threatened that his son, the son that he and Cathy brought into the world, will now spend the majority of his time with the man who split his marriage up.

Both seem to hold a reasonable position. Cathy wants to get on with building her new life away from a marriage that she has long thought of as dead and Daniel doesn't want to lose his son. The potential for conflict is obvious.

Steve and Hazel

Both Steve and Hazel recognised that their marriage had gone as far as it could and, although they were both sad, agreed that it would be far better to allow each other to form new relationships; they separated through mutual consent. They were also very clear that they would both continue to have a shared responsibility for their two children, Georgia, aged two, and David, aged five.

Hazel had been working part-time in a newsagent but, when she separated from Steve, she had to give up the job in order to look after the children as she could no longer afford childcare.

As she was now claiming state benefit, Steve was automatically assessed for child support by the Child Support Agency and was required to make a monthly payment to Hazel towards the care of the children.

Steve became angry about this because he was looking after the children for three nights of the week with no financial help from either the state or from Hazel – he had also been forced into debt in order to be able to move out of the family home.

Hazel, by contrast, was not only receiving a contribution from his earnings towards the care of the children but also had the child benefit book, received family tax credit and help towards the cost of her housing.

Steve felt that this was unfair and refused to pay his child support. Hazel was angry that Steve was withholding payment and refused to allow him to see the children.

In each of these cases, it is possible to see how both parents feel that they have right on their side and, equally, that both scenarios are ripe for long and bitter conflict.

Decision making

Think about the things that you and your partner may have disagreed about while you were parenting together. It may have been the times that your children went to bed, maybe it was whether they were allowed to have facial piercings or play certain types of video games.

It is fairly unreasonable to assume that these will simply melt away just because you no longer live together. In fact, not only will they not go away but they will be magnified to extreme proportions unless you are able to find a way to deal with them that you are both comfortable with.

Many parents who have been left with the responsibility of providing the majority of the hands-on care will take the view that the other parent has forfeited their right to a say. Indeed, many parents who feel that they have been wronged will actively allow things that were previously 'banned' in order to make it clear to the other parent that they no longer have a say in their children's upbringing.

The list of decisions and situations that are likely to be the cause of conflict are endless. For instance, where will the children's pet live after the separation? At whose house will the certificate for good school work be displayed? How will you divide up the journeys between the two family homes?

Equally, you will each have your own attitudes about what you think are the best ways to bring up your children. At what age is it appropriate to introduce advice on contraception? Is it wrong to feed the kids burgers and chips? How can you possibly let him walk around with holes in his jeans? Unless you both find strategies to negotiate your way through this new landscape, you will almost certainly find yourself on the long descent into conflict.

Conflict usually arises between couples when one person wants to see one particular outcome and the other person wants another. When you inhabit the same space, compromise becomes the only method of moving forward. In the separated family, however, decisions around parenting can be carried out away from each other and so the need for compromise is less obvious or immediately necessary. It would be a mistake, however, to assume that this means that compromise is no longer important. In many ways it becomes even more important if a perpetual war is not to break out between you and the other parent.

Let's look at a simple, everyday situation that may arise.

Stephanie

Six-year-old Stephanie lives for most of the week with her mother. On Saturday afternoons, she goes to her father's house. Stephanie's mother doesn't allow her to eat foods with a high sugar content as she has discovered that this makes Stephanie's behaviour difficult. Her father, nonetheless, persists in taking his daughter to the cinema where he buys her sweets and fizzy drinks. It is Stephanie's mother who has to deal with the little girl's tantrums, later on, in the evening.

In addition to making life difficult for Stephanie's mum, her father's unwillingness to compromise by, perhaps, buying Stephanie a different kind of food in order to give her a treat is inadvertently making Stephanie's life more difficult to negotiate; in the short term, she experiences her mum's anger at her behaviour, and in the long run, she is aware of the continued ill feeling between her mother and her father as a result of their inability to find a compromise.

One of the main barriers to reaching compromise is the, often, continued hostility between parents. This can mean that parents will actively do things that they know will upset or irritate the other parent, do things because they couldn't care less about how it affects the other parent or make independent decisions simply because they just can't face discussing it with the other parent.

We are not, by any means, advocating that every decision around your children's upbringing must be discussed with the other parent – indeed, one of the tasks of separating parents is to accept that the other person's way of parenting is valid (see Chapter 5) – but neither is it OK to go ahead regardless of how it affects the other parent.

And the reason for saying this is not because we are asking you to be nice to your former partner or even to consider their feelings. We are saying this because it is in the best interests of children to grow up in an atmosphere that is as free from conflict as possible.

The very basic thing that you need to agree on is that, whatever you think about each other, you will put the best interests of your children at the heart of every decision and action. Clearly, what each of you considers to be in the best interests of your children may not always coincide, but at least this offers a route out of conflict and into compromise. It will also demonstrate to your children that they are still prized by you both and that you are both willing to do the work to ensure that their childhood will be safe and happy.

Parenting values

That each of you may have different parenting values is likely to be a source of ongoing conflict. It is, therefore, a good idea to agree some basic ground rules by which you will each be able to assess both your own and the other parent's parenting decisions.

As each individual's values are as unique as their fingerprints, it would be foolish for us to try to provide a shopping list of things that you need to agree between you. However, it is a good idea for you both to write down the things that are important to you and also to begin by recognising the things that you already agree on.

Don't forget that, especially if you have been bringing up your child or children together for some time, you will, even if you haven't realised it, share many values in relation to parenting.

Think about and acknowledge those things that you both already agree on. Perhaps it is the time that your children go to bed, their religious or non-religious heritage, their diet, acceptable behaviours or even the number of hours that you feel it is OK for them to watch television.

By focusing first on the things that you already agree on, you can begin to work out what things may lead to conflict in the future. In fact, some of these areas of conflict may already have surfaced while you were living together.

Think about the things that really matter to you and make sure that you don't let feelings of anger or bitterness get in the way of being honest with yourself and the other parent. Don't forget that these are the values through which your children will be able to find a sense of continuity and security.

The way in which you reach an agreed set of basic values is entirely up to you. You may be able to sit down together and discuss them, or you may feel more comfortable writing to or emailing each other. You may decide to make a written record of your decisions or may find this too formal. Find what works for you both and then get on with it; there are more exercises in Chapter 6 to help you with this.

As a final tip, start with the positive (those areas that you both already agree on), express the things that are most important to you and agree where you can. If there are areas where agreement cannot be reached, find a compromise or find someone (a marriage guidance professional, for example) who may be able to help you.

Remember that children find security in the understanding that you are both fully engaged in their parenting and well-being.

Agreeing basic parenting values will help reduce conflict;

however, it is not a licence that allows you to interfere with the other parent's parenting decisions. In contrast, it should allow each of you to go off and parent separately, knowing that your children are in safe hands and will give you a tool to help you reach bigger decisions, which you may need to do together at some time in the future.

It is also vital for you both to recognise your child or children's changing needs as they grow. Those values that you bring to your parenting when your children are five years old may well not be appropriate when they are ten. For example, you may agree that your child should have a vegetarian diet at age five but acknowledge that, at age 12, your child is old enough to make a reasonably mature choice about the food that they wish to eat.

Conflict resolution

The first step towards managing anger and conflict is to understand and acknowledge the harm that it does to your children. A simple agreement that you can both make is that you will not argue or fight in front of the children. This is probably the single most important decision you will take, and it is one that will have lasting beneficial effects on your children.

It is a decision that each of you must be signed up to individually. In other words, you must be prepared to uphold your end of the bargain regardless of how the other parent behaves. The other parent starting an argument is not an invitation for you to join in. You must remain disengaged so that the children can see that they have, at least, one emotionally 'safe' parent in the situation.

It is conflict, not separation that harms children

The impact of shielding children from conflict, ensuring that they don't have to be witness to adult bitterness and anger, has immediate and significant results. All the research shows that it is the conflict that causes the scars, not the separation in itself.

Agree, between yourselves, a strategy for stopping arguments before they start. This doesn't mean taking the moral high ground or pointing out to the children how reasonable you are and how unreasonable the other parent is! It means finding a way that enables you both to step away from an argument knowing that any issues that need to be addressed can be revisited at a time and place when the children will not be present or witness to any disputes.

It's a difficult thing to ask two people who may have hurt one another, let each other down – people who may dislike, distrust and even fear each other – to continue to make decisions together about the most important people in their lives: their children. But it is because they are the most important people in your lives – because they require the security of your continued love and stability – that you will be prepared to do it.

Work at communication

Good communication can make life much easier for everyone and, if you can manage to establish methods of communication that you both feel comfortable with, the chances of conflict erupting are very much reduced.

If you consider the amount of information about your children that you shared when you were parenting together – things that have happened at school, worries or illnesses that they may have, who they were playing with, news about clubs they may have attended and outings they have been invited on – then it becomes clear that parenting apart will require a continued exchange of information.

Not only will it require continued exchanges of information, but if you are to reduce the likelihood of stressful situations and conflict, this flow of information needs to increase both in volume and detail. That's not easy given that it is likely that you'd rather not speak to the other parent at all unless it's absolutely necessary! A regular and businesslike exchange of information not only makes your life easier, it will also make your children feel a greater sense of security.

Own your own problems

'It's much better now that my mum and dad talk to each other about what me and my sister have been doing because it means that I don't have to say everything twice. I also know that they are both making sure that we don't get into trouble or anything.'

Ethan, aged 13

Given that we spend a good deal of every day communicating with other people, it would seem safe to assume that the skills we need to do this effectively come naturally. We can usually buy a newspaper or ask a friend if they fancy a trip into town without things getting too difficult. However, when we are looking to resolve problems, many of us lack even some of the basic insights into how best to proceed.

In situations where there is a problem, communications very easily run the risk of turning into conflict because neither party is able to identify clearly what the problem is or, where it is identified, who 'owns' it.

Being separated parents brings with it the added difficulty of not being able to separate out the essence of the problem from your negative feelings towards the other parent. In other words, it is easy to miss, or even deliberately cloud, the issue at hand because you want to make the other parent responsible for all the problems between you, as the following study illustrates.

Kate

As her parents are dropping in for a quick visit, Kate wants her son, Mark, at her house earlier than usual on Sunday evening so that they will be able to see him. She phones Mark's dad and asks, 'What time are you bringing Mark home?' He replies that it will be seven o'clock as usual.

Kate is angry and accuses Mark's dad of being inflexible. He retorts that this kind of irrational behaviour is typical of the reasons why they separated in the first place. The argument continues until Kate hangs up. Outcome – Kate is furious, Mark's dad is furious, Mark is bewildered and Kate's parents are disappointed.

Had Kate phoned Mark's dad and asked whether it would have been possible for her to collect Mark an hour earlier than usual as her parents would love to see their grandson, then the outcome could have been very different.

Kate would have 'owned' the problem (that her parents would not be able to see Mark unless the usual arrangements could be varied), Mark's dad would have been able to understand easily what it was that he was being asked to do and, with the situation being clear to everyone, Mark may well have had chance to see his grandparents.

Decide what you want from a situation and say it

If you want something to happen or want somebody to alter their behaviour, you need to express that clearly so that the other person is able to understand what is required of them. Don't be vague and then use the fact that you didn't get what you wanted to confirm for yourself how bad the other parent is!

For example, try saying: 'I feel' and say what you feel, 'when you' and describe the behaviour, 'because' and say how it affects you, 'What can we do about this?' and ask for a change in behaviour.

Or say 'I want' and say what you want, 'because' and explain why you want it, 'Are you able to do that?' and allow the other parent to say how they feel.

Top ten communication tips

You may need to learn new ways of communicating. Here are ten basic guidelines for minimising conflict while you are exchanging information:

1. **Focus only on the things that need to be resolved**
   Exchanges of information need to be businesslike and to the point. Focus on issues around the children, be specific and stick to the issue in hand. Try, wherever possible, to deal with one issue at a time or agree what points you wish to discuss in advance.

2. **Leave the past where it is** Don't get drawn into old battles. Once you have made the decision to separate, it is important to look forwards rather than backwards – what you are trying to achieve is a new parenting relationship for your children, not settle old scores.

3. **Avoid apportioning blame** The apportionment of blame does not make the communication of information any easier; it simply gets in the way. If there has been a problem, try to name it but then consider ways to prevent it reoccurring, away from the point of

exchange. Consider how your actions may have contributed to the problem as well as the actions of the other parent.

4. **Think about the language you use** Well-chosen language is the key to good communication. Keep your sentences short and avoid using accusatory phrases, such as 'You always' or 'You never'. Just stick to the matter in hand and state the facts as you see them. Saying, 'We agreed that bedtime should be nine o'clock' is far more effective and far less likely to end in conflict than 'You always let him stay up till midnight. You're determined to make him fail his exams, aren't you?'

5. **Leave family and friends out of it** It's never a good idea to support your arguments through other people. Don't use phrases like 'Ask Janet, she agrees with me' or 'Your sister always said you were like this.'

6. **Treat the other parent with respect** You may passionately dislike your former partner, you may never be able to forgive them for the hurt that they have caused you, but they are still 'mum' or 'dad' as far as your children are concerned. So try not to shout, abuse or insult the other parent – even if they are doing it to you – and make sure that your friends and family don't either. If you need to let off steam about the other person, do it away from your children.

7. **Listen properly** Ensure that you listen properly to what the other parent is saying. Make sure that they know you are listening and try your best not to interrupt them. Stay physically and emotionally engaged with the

discussion until it is finished. Unexpectedly with-drawing, walking out or putting the phone down will almost certainly increase tension between the two of you. If you are unhappy with the other parent's behav-iour, tell them what it is that you don't like, ask them to stop it and warn them that you are going to stop the conversation if they continue.

8. **Agree on the best times and places to talk** You may find it easier to talk face to face or you may both prefer the distance of a telephone call. Don't turn up unan-nounced at the other parent's house and never try to resolve issues under the influence of drugs or alcohol. You may find that meeting in a public place, such as a café, may reduce the likelihood of conflict.

9. **Don't make assumptions** Don't expect the other parent to be able to read your mind or assume that you can read theirs. It's important to be clear about why you believe a certain thing or have taken a particular action.

10. **Find a way to end your conversations** When you've dealt with the matters in hand, don't take the opportu-nity to stray off into other areas or return to old grievances. You will both experience a sense of control over your situation if you are able to bring your conver-sation to a successful conclusion. An agreed word, phrase or gesture will provide a useful signal.

Take responsibility for your own actions

Getting entrenched in conflict situations is one of the easiest things in the world to do. We feel a sense of injustice and we use it to excuse any actions we choose to take. It's the playground attitude of 'Well she/he started it!'

But you and the other parent can't allow your dealings with each other to remain in the playground. You are both adults and it is up to you both to act accordingly where your children are concerned. And if one parent is incapable of doing so in a particular situation, it means that it is even more important that the other parent does.

TIT-FOR-TAT RETALIATION

One situation that we encounter over and over again in our work is tit-for-tat retaliation between parents for things that they consider have been done to them. For example, mum has refused to allow her son to stay an extra night with his father so that they can go to the cinema together.

It may well be that this refusal was purely out of spite and a means to exercise control by denying an opportunity for dad to spend some extra time with his son doing something nice that the child wanted to do. In such a case, the refusal is negative and unhelpful and means that the boy misses out on seeing a film with his dad, an experience that the boy had been looking forward to.

The following week, mum asks if she can collect her son earlier in order for them to make the midday kick-off at the football team that they watch. Dad, remembering what happened the previous week, is absolutely not prepared to agree. He feels that he needs to stand his ground to make the point that flexibility has to work both ways and that he is not prepared to be pushed around by his son's mother.

As a result, the boy, having missed the film the previous week, now misses the football. Mum was wrong to refuse the extra night, but dad was equally wrong for refusing the earlier pick-up. In both cases, it is the boy who suffers.

If the father had agreed to the earlier pick-up, not only

would the boy have got to see the football, but it would have provided him with a model of responsible adult behaviour and may even have meant that mum might have been prepared to be more flexible in the future.

Disagreements about money may also erupt into disputes over things that are completely unrelated. For example, dad isn't making regular child support payments so mum stops their daughter seeing him, believing that if he isn't prepared to make the payments that he has been told to, then he has no right to see his daughter. This fails to recognise the girl as anything other than a bargaining counter and ignores her need and right to an ongoing relationship with her father regardless of the dispute over money.

Equally, dad is sick of getting no financial assistance for the two days a week that he looks after his son and decides that if the boy's mother is going to get all the financial help then she will have to do all of the caring – he stops seeing the boy. However angry the father is, he has to put this aside so that his son can grow up knowing that his father is a real and present adult in his life.

Children don't care about the transfer of money between parents, in fact, they rarely even know that it takes place. What they do care about is that their mum and dad discharge their parenting responsibilities without dragging them into disputes between the two of them.

If you need help, get it

Where you find that the other parent's behaviour towards you or your children fails to improve, you may need to get help from a third party. This may be informal, or you may need to enlist the help of family support practitioners, government agencies or solicitors. In all cases, though, you need to ensure that you are shielding your children from your disputes with the other parent and not using them as a way of getting the outcome that you desire.

Conclusion

This chapter has dealt with your relationship with your ex-partner and has, we hope, helped you to identify the things that you can do to help yourself on the way to disentangling yourself from your old relationship. We believe that this is vitally important if you are going to build a successful co-operative relationship because successfully dealing with all of the tasks of separation means that you will be more able to put your children's needs at the heart of your new parenting relationship.

It is unlikely that you will find it easy to disentangle yourself from the ties that have bound you to your former partner and your former life. Even where there is a sense of relief that a relationship has come to an end, many parents struggle with the process of psychological separation. There may well be other ties to consider, too: relationships with in-laws and extended families and also relationships with friends that you had in common. These things take time to work through and it can feel like a painful process, but the more you are able to separate, the better position you will be in to give your children what they need to adjust to the new situation.

Conflict, or the absence of it, is probably the single most important factor in how well children adjust to life after family separation. As parents, you both have a responsibility to avoid conflict wherever possible. By thinking about the things that are likely to lead to arguments before they arise, it is possible to develop strategies that mean that points of dispute or disagreement won't end in fights or longer-term, entrenched conflict.

By thinking about and learning new ways of communication, you will be able to develop skills and strategies that make conflict less likely. These will allow you to express your point of view more clearly and will mean that the chances of your children being caught up in a war between their parents are significantly reduced.

Think about how you may be contributing to any disputes between the two of you and try to think about things from the other parent's point of view. Above all else, consider what effect your actions will have on your children. Think about which is more important to you, getting your own way or keeping your children away from conflict. And if you find that you are running up against a brick wall and all attempts to deal with conflict are failing, get help.

Personal Story
Alex and Jamil – aged 34 and 38 – sharing care of their three children aged nine, eight and three

We are going to tell our story together because that's pretty much how we try and parent, still. It hasn't been easy getting to this point but because we were reasonably good friends throughout our separation and subsequent divorce, we have managed to achieve a pretty good way of living and looking after our children.

Alex: We separated when our youngest daughter was two years old. We were pretty much sure that the relationship had come to an end the year before, but we didn't want to let the children down. I was working for a dress designer and spending a lot of time in London during the week. Jamil was working at home and he looked after the school run and the shopping and after-school activities. I suppose that we just drifted in terms of our relationship. We had two children pretty soon after we were married and that was lovely. After that though we were working really hard to get Jamil set up in business and that was quite a pressure all round. When I got the opportunity to do this work for the design company we jumped at the chance because it brought in some extra cash just when we needed it.

I got pregnant with our youngest unexpectedly but that didn't mean that we were unhappy about it. I had put all the baby clothes away with all the baby things and it felt really nice to be getting them out again and looking forward to another little person coming along. I stopped working for the design company when I was eight months pregnant; I was pretty tired by then and ready for the rest. Of course I didn't get much of a rest as the baby was born two weeks early, although I managed a couple of weeks with my feet up before she arrived.

Jamil: It was a bit of a shock when Ellie arrived because the older two were, by then, at school and I had almost forgotten how hands-on a job it is having a newborn to look after. My business had just started to take off and I was trying to combine night feeds with early morning meetings which was a nightmare because sometimes I couldn't concentrate. Alex had a difficult time during the birth and it took a good three months for her to get back on her feet properly again. That meant that I was trying to get two kids off to school and a baby fed before I went off to my meetings; some mornings I could have cried it was such chaos. Alex got a lot stronger though in the next few months and took over most of the school runs, the shopping and general housekeeping.

Juggling the jobs that come with three kids though isn't easy and I know that Alex found it depressing and lonely a lot of the time. Anyway, by the time Ellie was a year old Alex wanted to get back to work. I was very reluctant to agree to this because I knew that it would mean a lot of nights away in London and that I would be back to combining work and round-the-clock child care. I wanted Alex to be happy though and I didn't want to hold her back so I agreed and she went back to work in September, two months after Ellie's first birthday.

From my perspective, it was a big mistake for Alex to go back to work that soon after Ellie was born. It meant that suddenly I was back in the middle of all the housework and that Alex would arrive home after a couple of days away just wanting to relax and unwind but there would be piles of washing to sort out and bags of shopping to unpack. It just didn't work and I got more and more exhausted and frustrated with it, and Alex just ended up not wanting to come home.

Alex: I would come home after a couple of days away and the house would be in total chaos. Sometimes it felt as if the kids were buried under the piles of washing or that they were just eating whatever they could grab out of the cupboard. I got really down and ended up never wanting to come home. Or I would come home and want Jamil to go out straight away so that I could sort the house out and get the kids fed and put to bed. It became a round of fighting and battling each other and it wasn't a marriage any more. We both knew, really, when I went back to work after Ellie that things weren't the same any more but it took another year before one of us was able to say this isn't working.

I was the one who moved out. I wanted to have my

own space and my own life. Of course I also wanted to have my children around me too, but I felt that they would be better off living in the big house with Jamil and spending part of every week with me. Culturally we have turned everything on its head. Jamil's heritage is Caribbean and there is this whole baby–father thing going on in that culture where women live with the kids and dads visit. Jamil though is part of the group of men who have challenged that way of being, which is very much his father's generation, and he was glad to stay in the house and be the main carer.

I moved just around the corner from Jamil into a three-bedroom flat. Of course we are very lucky to be able to afford to do that, which makes everything easier. We don't have to fight about money because we both earn our own living and we don't have to fight over who gets to stay in the house. We know that those things have really made a difference to the ways in which we have been able to be relaxed and comfortable about arrange-ments for the children.

Ellie spends a good deal of time with me here at the flat. She says she likes the flat better because it's smaller and she doesn't get lost! Also we are about three steps away from her nursery school here and she likes to be next door. The older two stick to a more regular pattern and come to me every other weekend from Friday until the following Thursday after school. If they need anything from home though they just call in and get it on the way to or from school.

I think the older two were more angry with me than Ellie, who was too small, really, to understand what was going on. Also, I took Ellie with me for the first weeks and she would go to see Jamil regularly. I think that was probably a mistake because they must have felt that I was choosing Ellie over them. Anyway they stick more to a routine and I think that's probably better for them as they can organise things like seeing friends and so on around that.

Jamil: I think we have managed to work things out so that the kids get the best out of the situation. It's fairly relaxed all round; the older two stick to their routine and Ellie just decides what she wants to do on a daily basis. She mostly spends her time at Alex's flat but she comes here whenever I make rice and peas, which are her favourite. We are only a year into this way of living and, therefore, still in the early stages. I sometimes wonder what will happen if one of us meets someone else. Will that upset the kids, for example, and how will I feel if there is another man around at Alex's? But for now it seems to work and the kids really do benefit from the relaxed arrangements, which is the most important thing of all.

Chapter 3

Your Children

'Your children are not your children. They are the sons and the daughters of life's longing for itself. They come through you, but they are not from you, and though they are with you, they belong not to you. You can give them your love but not your thoughts. They have their own thoughts. You can house their bodies but not their souls, for their souls dwell in a place called tomorrow, which you cannot visit, not even in your dreams. You can try to be like them. But you cannot make them just like you.'
Extract from *The Prophet* – Kahil Gibran

OVER THE PAST hundred years or so there has been an enormous change in family structures and the status of children within them. In the early days of the twentieth century, children were considered to be the property of their father primarily and then their mother. Children born into wealthier families were often expected to be educated until they took up their adult roles, while children living in poorer or uneducated families were expected to work for their keep from a very young age.

At the National Museum of Mining in Yorkshire there are tableaux depicting the life of a child in a working-class mining village in the mid-nineteenth century. This consisted of waking at 4.00 a.m. and eating a meagre meal, before accompanying mum and dad to the pit where the day was spent sitting in the pitch dark outside an area known as a gallery. Inside the gallery, which was a boarded-off room-sized space, older children alongside their mother and father would be hewing out lumps of coal from the coalface by hand. The only light within this space was a candle, which created an enormous risk of explosion from underground gas escapes. The role of the youngest child was, therefore, to sit outside the gallery and keep the door closed so that if there was an explosion, only the family inside would be killed. What an incredibly different experience of childhood this was, barely 150 years ago.

The advent of contemporary childhood really came about after the Second World War with the rise in interest in psychology and psychoanalysis. After the war, child psychologists, such as Dr Spock, were publishing books advising parents how to bring up their children; and psycho-analysts, such as D.W. Winnicott, were suggesting theories, such as maternal deprivation as a source of the problems of childhood.

In the twenty-first century, we continue the debate about childhood. What is a good childhood, what does childhood mean, what is the purpose of childhood? This debate is nowhere more focused than when it is about family separa-tion and its impact on children. Does family separation ruin childhood, interrupt childhood, change childhood? If so, does it automatically lead to delinquency, teenage preg-nancy, difficulties in forming relationships in adulthood or inevitable separation and divorce for children themselves?

The answer is that separation and divorce do not in them-selves lead to any of the problems listed above. However, the ways in which parents handle separation and divorce may affect children positively or negatively. The key to helping children cope is held by parents and those other important adults in children's lives, such as grandparents, aunts and uncles, and friends of the family. All of these people have the power to influence, positively or negatively, the ways in which children are affected by separation and divorce. It is incumbent upon all of us to use this power wisely because, as we will go on to discuss in this chapter, successfully coping with parental separation and divorce reduces the chance of experiencing them later in life.

Since the early 1970s there has been a steady rise in the incidence of separation and divorce. With the women's movement came a greater freedom to choose whether or not to remain in a marriage that was not working, and with the change in the law that had hitherto prevented mothers who left marriages from taking children with them, the increase in divorce continued apace.

At the start of the twentieth century, most children were unlikely ever to experience family separation and divorce and just as unlikely to know any other children whose parents were separated or divorced. By the end of the century, however, around nine children out of every class of 30 will have had direct experience of family separation. The experience of family separation is all around us too: in newspaper reports, soap operas and children's television programmes. This means that the experience of family separation is not something that children will be completely unfamiliar with. That doesn't mean that it won't have a huge impact on children if their own parents decide to separate or divorce.

What family life means to children

Families are the people who are important in children's lives from the earliest days and weeks. These people may be biologically related to the children or not. There may be one important person in a baby's early days or there may be many. What is important about the early days of a baby's life is that he or she is able to form secure attachments to those people who will be their regular carers.

What parents provide

It used to be thought that mothers were the most important person to care for a baby and that this was somehow biologically determined. Studies have shown, however, that while mothers are one of the most important people for a baby to be with, fathers and other carers can be equally important. The nature versus nurture debate rages most fiercely around these early days with many people continuing to believe that a baby needs its mother and that father care comes second best.

What is important to a baby, however, is not whether the arms holding him or her are male or female, or the voice speaking is high or low, but that the arms are there whenever discomfort overwhelms and the voice is heard in response to cries of distress or alarm. Smells, too, are important to a baby and if the skin of the person smells familiar, then the baby will feel soothed and safe. Later, a baby will begin to establish eye contact and later still will be able to differentiate between faces; but for now, in the early days, what matters is the consistency of responses and familiarity of being soothed whenever distress arises.

Family life for young children is the experience of being

important to a group of people and having their emotional and physical needs taken care of by adults. Families provide a place in which a baby can grow into a toddler and start to venture out to explore the world immediately beyond the protective arms that once soothed distress away. As long as those protective arms are still there on a consistent basis whenever danger is felt, toddlers can start to explore the world around them freely and begin to make sense of their separateness from the adults who take care of them.

Different kinds of family

Families come in all shapes and sizes. In the UK, the nuclear family is still the most predominant structure; however, there are also cultural differences in the structure of families with some consisting of grandparents, aunts and uncles too, all living under the same roof. In some households, one parent and their children form a family. Sometimes this is the way the family has lived from the birth of a baby, sometimes this way of living is the result of family separation. Children living in separated family situations will often be a part of two or more different family units and will learn to negotiate their way from one to another. More of this later.

The important thing to recognise about families is that there is no right or wrong family structure and no one structure is better than the other. What matters about families is that they offer the people who live in them safety, continuity, warmth and affection, as well as boundaries and guidelines within which all can feel secure. It is the responsibility of the adults who form the family unit to establish and maintain these conditions so that children who are living in the family unit can grow and learn about relationships and responsibilities. We learn to be parents in the early days of being parented ourselves, and as we will see later in this chapter, the quality of our early experiences of being parented has a profound effect upon us for the rest of our lives.

Children and attachment

In order to feel secure in themselves throughout childhood and beyond, children need to achieve what is called a secure attachment. Put simply, in order to feel secure about ourselves, we need to have an internal sense of safety that we can draw upon throughout our life. This internal safety is built in our early childhood in our relationship with our early caregivers.

As babies grow into toddlers they begin to experience what is called separation anxiety. This is the awareness that survival is dependent upon another human being and that this person is not always present. Until the toddler is able to understand that someone who is out of the room still exists and will come back, anxiety on separation from caregivers is likely. Separation anxiety happens because young children have a limited ability to think beyond the immediate time frame they are experiencing.

Life for young children is what happens in the here and now, and they are at first unable to understand that someone who is not there will return. Eventually, however, if primary caregivers are able to demonstrate reliably and consistently that they do return, the young child will develop an internal awareness of that fact and will begin to build an ability to find security in that awareness. This is what is called a secure attachment.

Separation anxiety

For young children separation anxiety is a very real issue, and cultures across the world acknowledge this through the fairy stories and fables that are told to young children. Stories, such as *Hansel and Gretel* and *Babes in the Wood*, illustrate the terror of parental loss that is a child's biggest fear. The happy endings of tales, such as these, offer children the reassurance that they need that all will end well for them too whenever their fear of being abandoned arises.

Separation anxiety fades as children begin to develop an internal sense of constancy in their relationships with their early caregivers. This happens at around the time that children are starting school. Providing that a child's needs have been taken care of reliably and consistently, by the time they start school they are able to let go of their caregiver for short periods, confident in the knowledge that they will return. A child who has a secure sense that their caregiver will return is said to have a 'secure attachment'. As human beings we are born with a predisposition to form attachment bonds – our survival depends upon it.

ATTACHMENT BONDS

These bonds are built in the relationship between a child and its primary caregivers with interactions, such as smiles and holding eye contact, which are designed to elicit ongoing warmth and affection on the part of each. A baby aged four weeks will prefer the smell of its primary caregivers and by eight weeks will hold eye contact with these people. By the age of three months a baby will be able to differentiate between the faces of its primary carers and other adults, and will readily smile.

By the age of six to nine months the smiles will become more selective and be aimed primarily at the caregivers.

Attachment by this stage has deepened and the baby will have a preference for a circle of familiar faces. These care-givers will now be able to elicit smiles and positive reactions readily, but will also be the cause of much distress when they leave. Repeated return when there is distress will soothe the separation anxiety being experienced until the child grows older, and strengthens the internal attachment. Infants who are secure within themselves are more confident and have been shown to have a higher self-esteem than those who display more insecure attachments.

Attachment bonds last a lifetime, and it therefore makes sense that these need to be securely felt from an early age. Secure attachment bonds between children and their primary caregivers ensure that relationships are strong and that the warmth, love and affection felt within them are enduring.

Such is the importance of the attachment bonds that we continue to seek close relationships with other people throughout our lives. How securely attached we are to our own parents will also, in turn, affect how we are able to parent our own children. If we were responded to regularly and were able to seek and obtain our parents' attention and care when we needed it and not just when our parents felt like providing it, we will be more likely to be able to offer our children the consistency of having their needs met on their terms rather than our own.

The impact of family separation on children's attachment

The ways in which the actuality of the separation occur can temper the impact of family separation on children. The impact will also be different for children at different ages. The biggest impact will be upon young children who experience one of their parents suddenly moving out of the family home. Children who are not prepared for this will often display an immediate and acute return to separation anxiety, displaying symptoms such as bed-wetting, clinginess and extreme distress whenever the parent who remains leaves the room. Older children who have not been prepared for the departure of one of the parents may become withdrawn, angry or hostile towards the parent who remains in the family home.

One of the key things to help children is, therefore, preparation for the departure of one of the parents from the family home. Preparation for departure will include talking with children, describing to them how they will continue to be with the parent who is leaving on a regular basis and how the love that each parent has for their children will continue regardless of the fact that mum and dad will be living in separate homes.

Children should not be left to guess what is happening to their parents' relationship. In these circumstances children will make up stories to explain to themselves what is going on. Children are always trying to make sense of things that they do not understand, and it is far better for them to receive clear and honest explanations that they can understand rather than being left to make sense of things themselves. It is no good assuming that children will have anticipated the separation because there have been lots of arguments recently, for example. Young children can still be completely unaware of the potential for family separation even in the most toxic environment. Older children may be more prepared, but they will also appreciate and respect parents more if the impending plans for separation are laid out clearly for them and discussion is encouraged about how the relationship with the departing parent will continue.

From the day that the actual physical separation occurs the departing parent should begin a routine of regular contact with their children. A daily phone call at bedtime is useful for younger children, particularly if the departing parent was the person who read bedtime stories or took care of the bedtime routine. A regular time for saying goodnight could be set up and the phone call needs only to be short, focusing upon what has happened at school and ending with a reassurance of when the next phone call or visit will be. The parent who is at home with the child can then take over and continue to reassure the child that all is well and that the other parent will be there the next day for them and the day after that.

For older children a regular time to talk is important but it may not need to be daily. At first, however, it is probably useful for all children to know that they can have daily contact with the parent who has left the home.

Preparation is needed before the physical separation takes place; this should include a clear and honest explanation of what is going to happen (it needs to be appropriate for the age of the children). For older children, a discussion should be had about ongoing relationships and how these will be facilitated. Children of all ages risk a return to separation anxiety so be prepared for clinginess, bed-wetting and other regressive behaviours. A new routine for regular (daily at first) contact between children and the parent who is leaving the family home should be set up from the day of departure.

Preparing children for family separation

It is always useful to try to think through how you are going to tell children that you are separating. The phrase 'we will always be your mum and dad' is often used and it is assumed that children understand the sentiment behind that.

Many children, however, will not understand what that

means and will need a much clearer explanation of how you will continue to be mum and dad if you no longer live in the same house together or if you are not living with your children. Telling children that they will speak to dad every day on the phone before bedtime while they are with mum, and that when they are at dad's house on Monday, Tuesday and Wednesday nights they will speak to mum at bedtime is a much better way of describing how you will continue to be mum and dad.

Older children should be consulted about the arrangements for living with one parent or the other; however, this is not always possible if there is a great deal of conflict between parents or where one parent does not want the separation and is obviously distressed by the impending departure of the other. In these circumstances children often unconsciously take sides, and it is, therefore, more appropriate to have an agreement between parents beforehand about the living arrangements for the children. This means that the children can be consulted but also discouraged from taking sides, and parents can demonstrate that they are the people who are responsible for the changes in the family and that they are old enough to care for themselves without needing the children to do it for them.

Be prepared for separation anxiety

Separation anxiety returns whenever children experience a fear that they may be abandoned. Even with the best preparation, some children will feel this fear even if they cannot articulate it verbally. It is important, therefore, that both parents look out for signs and symptoms of separation anxiety and offer the reassurance that children are seeking: that they are not going to be abandoned by either parent. Signs of separation anxiety vary from child to child but are mainly concerned with a child regressing into behaviour that they had previously grown out of. Bed-wetting, thumb-sucking and taking up abandoned 'comfort' objects, such as a favourite toy, blanket or an item of clothing, are all signs of separation anxiety. Crying and being clingy when going to school or being taken to nursery are also signs of anxiety returning, and any child who was previously happy to go to school and now shows signs of worry about being left is definitely experiencing separation anxiety.

Separation anxiety can be very difficult to deal with, and for parents who are just starting to share care of children or spend parenting time with them after separation, it can make the whole experience pretty miserable. It's not much fun, either, for children who are having to deal with some powerful feelings that they neither understand nor have control over. The following study exemplifies this.

Jack and Nina

Alice is the seven-year-old daughter of Jack and Nina who have recently separated. Alice lives with Nina and sees Jack every week on Wednesday night and every other weekend from Saturday lunchtime to Sunday evening. This arrangement has been in place for about two months but it is getting increasingly difficult for both parents because of Alice's repeated distress each time she is due to be dropped off at Jack's house.

Alice becomes so distressed and agitated during the trip to Jack's house that Nina is starting to worry that the time she spends with Jack is doing her some harm; Jack is starting to feel as though he is causing damage to Alice by having her to stay with him. Fortunately Jack and Nina are reasonably friendly. If they were not, it would be remarkably difficult for them to tease out the reason for Alice being so distressed.

Talking to Alice doesn't shed much light on the problem; when each parent asks her directly if she wants to keep going to her daddy's house, she says yes and is really keen to say what she likes about going there. When she is picked up by Nina, she always says she has had a really good time.

Nina has also noticed that Alice is starting to get upset on the way to her ballet lessons and sometimes she gets upset when she goes to school in the morning. Her teachers say that she settles down fairly quickly but Nina is worried about Alice clinging to her while they are waiting for the bell to go instead of running off to play with her friends like she used to. A visit to the GP turns up nothing but the GP suggests that Nina talk to one of the practice child psychologists about Alice's behaviour.

The child psychologist asks Nina about recent changes in Alice's life, and Nina explains that she and Jack have recently separated and that Jack has gone to live in a new home. The psychologist explains to Nina that what Alice is experiencing is called separation anxiety and that her dad leaving home has brought it about. The psychologist also explains that while Alice is able to articulate her positive feelings about seeing her dad and spending time with him regularly, she cannot verbalise her negative fears. This is because these are located in her unconscious and she is, therefore, only able to act them out rather than talk about them.

The clinginess and agitation on being left by her mother at school, at ballet lessons and at her father's are Alice's expressions of her unconscious fear that her mother will not return to collect her. As one parent has left home, Alice is afraid that her mother will also disappear out of her everyday life and that she will be utterly abandoned.

Understanding how children demonstrate their unconscious fears can unlock some of the frustrating battles that occur when adults do not know what to do with a child who is distressed but cannot say why. Understanding that Alice is not consciously afraid of being abandoned, but has regressed into a younger state of being, can offer Nina and Jack the information that they need to build strategies for helping Alice. By thinking through the situation from Alice's perspective, Jack and Nina were able to make some minor changes that were extremely beneficial for Alice.

For example, instead of Nina dropping Alice off at Jack's house each time, Jack began to collect Alice from school on Wednesdays and Nina collected her from Jack's house later on. This meant that the experience of being left somewhere was reduced for Alice and that her experience of seeing her father was that he came to collect her from school. On Saturdays, Jack began to collect Alice from Nina's house after which they would go straight to the park or do some other activity which distracted Alice from the transition. On Sundays, Nina collected Alice at the usual time; it was at this transition time that the separation anxiety still showed itself with Alice being distressed at leaving her father behind.

Jack tried dropping Alice off at Nina's house for a couple of weeks, and each parent concentrated upon reassuring Alice that she would see the other parent again at the usual time. In addition to this, Jack and Nina agreed that Alice would call Jack to say goodnight every day that she wasn't with him which would provide continuity of contact and more reassurance for her. After three months, Alice began to settle down again and her clingy behaviour and distress disappeared. Having understood the psychology of separation anxiety, Nina and Jack were able to offer Alice the reassurance that she needed in order to be able to accept and deal with the change in her life circumstances.

Establishing reassuring routines

From the first day of the separation children will need re-assuring routines that demonstrate that both parents will continue to meet their emotional and physical needs. Whereas it may feel difficult to talk about this at the point of separation, being able to do so and set these in place will have a long-lasting positive impact upon children. The parent who will be living with the children for most of the time, or, where caring is going to be shared more equally, the parent who will be with the children on the day of the physical separation, should take responsibility for making sure that there is quiet space for children to talk if they need to or to simply just be with the parent if they don't want to talk.

The physical upheaval of one parent moving out of the house will have an impact on children. Some parents arrange things so that their children are not at home when the move happens. This is not always a good idea, especially if the children have not been properly prepared. The ideal situation is for children to be involved in the move with the parent who is leaving, visiting the place where that parent is going to live and perhaps even spending some time in the first week with that parent helping to unpack and make the space home. Children do not like seeing their parents unhappy or alone and often want to accompany parents so that they can make them feel better.

If you feel too upset or distressed by the move, it is not a good idea to involve children in it, but if you are able and are moving into a place where you will live with your children on a weekly basis, letting them help out will establish a sense of belonging and participation in your new life for your children right from the start.

Establishing new routines if a new partner is involved

New partners are the only issue that we are prescriptive about. We believe, emphatically, that you should not involve your children in any new relationship at the point of family separation. It doesn't matter whether you think that your new partner is the best thing that ever happened in your life, your children are very unlikely to share your view at this point. This means that if you are moving in with a new partner or you have a new partner and your ex-partner is moving out, your relationship with that new person should be kept well away from your children until they have dealt with the impact of the separation and you are reasonably certain that the new relationship is going to last.

You should certainly not expect to involve your children in any new relationship within the first two years after family separation. They deserve time to recover from the loss of their family unit and to adjust to new ways of being. You may want to be involved with another person but that does not mean that they want to be or that they will benefit from that. On too many occasions we have been approached by parents whose children are showing behavioural difficulties in day-to-day life and are having problems at school too.

At the heart of these difficulties often lies grief and sadness about the break-up of the family, and anger and frustration at being forced to build relationships with people that they consider to be strangers or interlopers in their lives.

Being your children's parent is your first and foremost responsibility and, we would argue, after family separation it should be your primary consideration for the first two to three years. If you are involved with someone new at the point of family separation and you are moving in with that person, do not expect your children to want to visit you at that home and share their time with you and your new partner. Do not expect, either, that your children will understand why you have left them to live with another person.

Children can, in time, adjust to new people in your life, but they will not take kindly to being expected to accept your new partner as their step-parent within days of you moving out. Similarly, if your ex has moved out because you are having a relationship with someone new and your children are living with you, do not expect to be able to move that person into your home within a short period of time without it affecting your children negatively.

You may wish to live with your new partner, they almost certainly will not. It doesn't matter how caring or nice your new partner is, children need and deserve the time to adjust to the separation of their parents before they are asked to adjust to the presence of another person in your life. If you are in a new relationship at the point of family separation heed these instructions if you do nothing else – keep your new relationship separate from your relationship with your children and allow time for everyone to adjust to the change before you try and establish a new family life.

Helping children to deal with family separation

Anger, sadness, worry, relief, confusion, guilt, embarrassment, loneliness, nervousness – these are all common emotions that children experience when their parents sep-arate. Many children have difficulty expressing these emotions in words.

Drawing pictures

An easier way for children to express how they really feel inside can be by drawing pictures of feelings. Drawing helps children express themselves in a positive manner and also helps parents to get a better understanding of what their children are thinking and feeling concerning the separation. After your children have drawn a picture, ask specific questions about the drawing. Encourage them to explain what they have drawn and why; be positive and supportive.

Suggest to your children that they could draw pictures to describe the following:

- What does separation look like?

- How does separation make you feel?

- Various feelings, such as anger, sadness or loneliness.

- Their family, including anyone they feel is part of the family. Write each person's name by his or her picture.

- A picture of the homes they live in.

- If a genie could grant them one wish related to their family, what would they wish for?

Communicating from a distance

When one parent moves a considerable distance away, coping with the separation often becomes more difficult for children because, in addition to the effects of the separation, they must also adjust to not seeing that parent very often. The following tips can help parents and children maintain strong relationships from long distances:

- Email each other. Email is a fast, convenient way to keep in touch.

- Start a postcard club. Everyone likes to receive mail. It only takes a few minutes to fill out a postcard. Give some stamped cards to your children and take turns sending a card each week.

- Have weekly or monthly phone dates. Set a specific time when you will talk on the phone (for example, Wednesday evenings at 7.00 p.m. or the first Sunday of each month at noon). This will give both of you something to look forward to.

- Create a shared journal. Buy an inexpensive notebook and write your thoughts and feelings in it. Exchange the notebook when you see each other.

- Create a family website. This is a great way to post information and pictures to each other.

- Make audio or video tape recordings. Hearing or seeing each other, whether for special occasions or just during daily activities, will keep the bond between you strong.

Letter writing

Writing letters is a constructive way to deal with confused feelings and to let off steam. Encourage your children to write letters to the other parent, expressing their feelings about the separation. Tell them they can write whatever they feel like. Assure them that they do not have to send the letters if they do not want to. The act of putting feelings and ideas in writing often helps to put the situation in perspective.

These are some ideas to include in a letter.

Dear Mum,

I am really angry that you left us without saying goodbye properly.

I am sad that you are not here when I come in from school.

I am afraid you don't care about me any more.

I am sorry I shouted at you when you came back to get your bags.

I love you and I want you in my life.

Love, Billy

Parent information cards

Make information cards for you, your children and the other parent. Write information about yourself on one side of a large index card and put information about your children's other parent on the other side. With this card, you, your children and your children's other parent will always know how to contact each other.

Items to include:

- Name

- Addresses (home and work)

- Phone numbers (home and work)

- Days I live with this parent

- Things we like to do together

Reading children's books

Many children's books address the topic of separation. Reading such books with your children can be a valuable way to help them work through the feelings and concerns they are facing regarding the separation in their own lives; children often identify with characters in books. Discussing how characters work through their challenges can give your children insight into their own situation.

Writing stories

Many children write and illustrate stories. If your children enjoy this kind of activity, suggest that they write a story about separation. Encourage them to be as creative as possible and to draw pictures that help illustrate the story. If your children are willing, have them share their story with you. Be sure to be positive and supportive of their work.

Personal history timeline

One common feeling children experience after the separation is worry about the future. They may be concerned about what is going to happen to them and if their lives will ever be normal again. Creating a timeline can help children put the current events of their lives into perspective. It can help them see that they have experienced many good things in the past, and that they have many years ahead of them to have fun and happy times with their families. Younger children will need help with this activity but will enjoy thinking of events for their parent to put on their timeline. Discuss your children's timeline with them when they have finished. Point out that they have experienced many different events throughout life, some good and some bad. Help them to understand that they can get through the difficult time of separation and that there are good times and happiness ahead.

DIRECTIONS FOR A PERSONAL HISTORY TIMELINE:

- Draw a long horizontal line on a sheet of paper.

- Label your birth at one end with a star.

- Label the present time somewhere in the middle.

- Mark significant events that have occurred in your life between the 'birth' star and the 'present' mark. Possible ideas include births of siblings, getting pets, starting school, moving, learning to read, learning to ride a bike, separation, divorce, remarriage, joining a team or club, death of relatives and special holidays and vacations.

- Mark events that you hope will happen in the future.

Playing together

As with drawing pictures, play is often a good way to help children express their feelings when it is difficult to talk about them. The following are some ideas of effective play activities:

- **Make puppets** Create finger puppets or puppets out of brown paper bags. Have the puppets talk about their feelings.

- **Play games** Sometimes when people are occupied in another activity, it is easier to talk about feelings than if they just sit down to have a talk. There are even some games on the market that specifically address separation.

- **Role play** Practise dealing with difficult situations that come about during separation by acting out scenarios and discussing ways these situations can be handled positively.

Exercise together

Engaging in physical activities together helps parents and children spend time with one another and reap the health benefits of exercise. Exercising is a good way to get rid of tension or angry feelings in a positive way.

Activities to enjoy together include:

- Swimming

- Biking

- Hiking

- Walking

- Camping

- Fying kites

- Rollerblading

Creating two comfortable homes

Your children should feel comfortable both in your home and in the home of your former partner. Making sure that each home contains familiar items will help your children feel secure and at home in both places. Involve your children in planning what will be in both houses and, if possible, work with your children's other parent. Think about including the following items in both households:

- Favourite toys and games

- Basic school supplies (paper, pencils, scissors, and so on)

- Clothing (underwear, socks, pyjamas, jeans, and so on)

- Toiletries (toothbrush, hairbrush, deodorant, and so on)

- Favourite foods

- Photos of all family members

Time capsule

Making a time capsule is another way of helping children recognise that the troublesome feelings surrounding the separation won't last for ever and that there are many things to look forward to in the future. Have your children put things in the capsule that represent their lives: stories, drawings, photographs and other special treasures and reminders. Encourage your children to write down answers to the following questions and include them in the time capsule:

- Who are your friends?

- Who is part of your family now?

- Who will be part of your family in the future?

- Where will you be living in one year? Five years?

- What kinds of things do you like to do?

- What would you like to learn how to do in the future?

- What do you want to be when you grow up?

There are many different kinds of containers that make good time capsules – large glass jars with tight lids, large manila envelopes, shoeboxes or drawstring bags. After your children have finished making the time capsule, help them seal it. Let them decide when they will open it. For example, it might be opened in one year, on a certain birthday, or five years from the separation. When the time comes to open the capsule, your children will undoubtedly have fun looking at the things they put in it, noticing how their handwriting has changed, and reading the things they wrote.

Things to watch out for

There are some things that children experience that it is useful to watch out for in the early days after family separation. These are not always obvious and it can take some careful detective work to discover them. Children do not always have the ability to verbalise their feelings, particularly younger children. This means that quite often what you will notice will be unusual behaviour or patterns of thinking that make themselves known through the questions that your children might ask you, sometimes about things that are completely unrelated to the separation.

When you, yourself, are experiencing grief after the ending of a relationship or are immersed in the changes in your lifestyle or routine, it can be easy to miss signs that your children are struggling with the change too. It is worth, therefore, talking to grandparents, aunts, uncles and friends about things they could watch out for when they are spending time with the children. These extended family members and friends will have their own issues to deal with in relation to the separation but they should be at least one step away from the immediate feelings of grief, anxiety or distress. It is also worth talking to your children's other parent about the things that children might be experiencing and, where possible, keeping each other informed about anything that may be worrying children particularly.

Reunification fantasies

One of the strongest fantasies that children of all ages have about their separated parents is that they will eventually get back together again. Even adult children of separated parents experience this fantasy, which can manifest itself as anger towards the parent who instigated the separation and taking sides with the other parent. Younger children might verbalise their reunification fantasies; Lauren, aged four, told her father that she 'would like to put a rope around mummy and drag her back home again'. Others might act out their fantasies while they are playing with dolls or friends.

Reunification fantasies can be powerful for children and are part of the Change Curve, which is explained in Chapter 1. Reunification fantasies are part of the disbelief section of the curve and, as such, are a form of denial that the separation has occurred.

One of the problem things to look out for when children experience reunification fantasies is that they are taking it upon themselves to try, physically, to reunite their parents. Signs that this kind of thing is happening might be when they ask if dad can read a bedtime story when they are dropped off or if dad can sleep over to make sure that they are OK in the night. Any attempt by children to re-establish old routines can be part of a fantasy about reunification. While it is perfectly acceptable for dad to read a bedtime story on occasion and overnight stays are OK if parents are amicable and comfortable with that arrangement, it is not a good idea to give in to repeated pleas for daddy to stay or read bedtime stories on a longer-term basis.

Reunification fantasies are normal for every child whose parents have separated, but they are fantasies and parents need to help them to be resolved by maintaining firm but reassuring boundaries around the change in living arrangements and routines. Nothing will confuse a child more than parents who give in to pleas at night only to resume the separate way of living the next day.

Taking responsibility for the separation

Children who experience reunification fantasies often take on responsibility for either the separation itself or their inability to repair and reunify their parents' relationship. Signs that a child is taking responsibility in this way can be detected through anxiety about whether they are loved or lovable enough.

How boys and girls react at different ages

All children are upset by their parents' separation at first and during the first year will show signs of fear, anger, guilt and depression. By the second year however these reactions are usually diminished. Where reactions continue beyond the first year or during the first year appear unusually intense, it may be useful to see a child psychologist for some assistance on helping your child to deal with how they are feeling.

Very young children

It used to be a widespread assumption that babies and toddlers could not be affected by family separation because they are too young. However, it is clear from studies that young children are affected by change in routines and that most will demonstrate a reaction to this. Given that attachment bonds are being formed during the early weeks and months of a child's life, any change in the lives of the people to whom the child is becoming attached will affect the child. This is because a child's sense of self is formed in the attachment process, which is the interaction between caregivers and their children.

Recent studies have also shown that a child's sense of well-being or level of contentment is formed in the relationship. Our sense of well-being and contentment depends upon the feel-good hormone serotonin, the production of which is governed by the part of the brain that is busy during the attachment process. Studies have shown that it is the caregiver's smiles and positive reactions to the baby that kick-start the production of serotonin in the brain and that it is the level of serotonin production that gives rise to a sense of contentment and well-being in the baby. Depressed caregivers, or those who are experiencing grief and sadness after family separation, may not be able to offer the baby the kind of interaction needed to kick-start the production of serotonin. A baby may be cognitively unaware that its parents have separated but it will, nonetheless, be affected by the change.

Preschool children (two to five years old)

Children of this age group often react with both anger and sadness, and both sexes tend to cry more often and be more demanding. This is the age when separation anxiety affects children most profoundly; therefore, the loss of the daily input of one of their parents or a significant change in routine will have a powerful impact upon them.

Boys of this age tend to become angrier and more restless. They may withdraw from friends and sit on their own more or they may disrupt group activities.

Girls at this age also become angry although some become little adults, taking care of themselves and becoming overly concerned with being clean and neat. Both girls and boys can become insecure about the other parent leaving, and it is at this age that bed-wetting and other regressive behaviour may be apparent.

Primary school children (six to eight years old)

Family separation is particularly difficult for this age group. The main reaction for boys and girls is sadness and both sexes can be openly weepy. At this age children are most vulnerable to thinking that their parents have rejected them, which can lead to low self-esteem and feelings of being unloved and unlovable.

This is the age during which a drop in performance at school is likely and disruptive behaviour in the classroom a regular occurrence, particularly for boys. Depression is a risk for children in this age group and concerns over parents as well as reunification fantasies are strong. Boys in this age group are likely to be more distressed than girls if their father leaves home, and may miss him intensely.

Primary school children (nine to 11 years old)

This group experiences anger more than any other emotion, and children can be intensely angry with one or both parents during and after family separation. Children of this age tend to take sides against the parent who initiated the separation and want to apportion blame. This can make children susceptible to destructive parental games where one parent is trying to blame the other or get revenge.

Anger, however, is not their only reaction; children of this age group are often very concerned with their parents' welfare, frightened about what is going to happen to them and can be very lonely. They can feel powerless and experience an intense desire for their parents to get back together again. Mostly they experience a strong wish for things to be back to normal and for the changes to have not happened.

About half of the children in this age group will suffer a drop in performance at school as concentration and confidence are badly affected. Some will also start to experience their emotional distress as psychosomatic illness and start to complain of headaches, stomach aches, constipation perhaps, and sometimes nightmares and sleepwalking.

Children of this age can also try to take care of the parent with whom they are living, acting like parents themselves and trying to make things better for the adult.

Boys are susceptible to withdrawn behaviour and acting badly. Mothers of boys in this age group might find discipline difficult and fathers who do not live regularly with their sons may find attempts to spend time with them are rejected.

Adolescents (12 years and upwards)

How adolescents react varies greatly and depends upon where they are in their progress through puberty. Some react much better than younger children; this is because they have achieved some independence and separation from their parents and do not need as much affection and guidance as younger children.

Some adolescents react by focusing upon their own ambitions and plans and distance themselves from the problems that their parents are having. They may worry about how a separation will affect their future, whether they will have to move schools, for example, or whether separation is going to mean that there is less money in the family for their growing needs. Just like younger children, adolescents are vulnerable if they feel that they are being pulled into loyalty conflicts and asked to take sides with one parent against the other.

Some adolescents do not cope well with family separation and feel betrayed by their parents. Some disengage from their family and spend more time with their friends away from home. If this is accompanied by a lack of supervision by parents, adolescents are at risk of becoming involved in misuse of alcohol or drugs during this period, or find themselves failing at school or involved in risky behaviour, including underage sexual activity.

Infrequently and almost exclusive to girls in this age group there can be a positive developmental response to family separation. Girls can show maturity and take part in helping parents to care for younger children or help with the household. This, however, can be something to watch out for if it goes on too long or means that the girl is forgoing fun with friends or getting behind with school work. This response can mean that the girl is avoiding her adolescent life in order to try to repair the problems of the adults in her life.

Things to keep in mind about boys' and girls' reactions to family separation

Do not expect your children to carry on as normal. Children react to family separation in different ways but most will need time to grieve and come to terms with what has happened. Every child is an individual and the responses shown above are generalised. An emotionally mature or immature child may react in ways similar to the group above or below their age group. Personality, a child's place in the family and their relationship with each parent will have an impact on how a child deals with family separation.

We cannot protect our children from the grief of family separation or other grief, such as the death of a pet, a beloved grandparent or when best friends move away. Helping children to deal with the grief of family separation in a way that enables them to express it and come to terms with change will give them emotional skills for life.

Helping to make it easier for children

This section covers the things that you can do for your children that will make the transition to life in a separated family easier for them. Most children need help in coming to terms with what has happened to their family, and it is, therefore, important that you think about the practical ways that you can offer support to them.

Talking to children

Children differ in their response to family separation. Some children will want to ask lots of questions, others will not want to talk at all about what has happened. At some point, however, you will need to talk to your children about what is going to happen in terms of the family living separately and how you feel about this. It can be very difficult simply to sit children down and announce that you are going to be living in different homes. In our experience, younger children don't really understand what is happening until the change is under way and older children, particularly teenagers, can become monosyllabic whenever they are asked formally to sit down and listen to an announcement (particularly if it's going to be something they suspected and don't want to hear).

The best way to talk to children about what is happening or going to happen is when you have a lot of time spare to spend with them. Talking to younger children about what is going to happen while you are doing something with them, such as baking a cake or cutting and sticking pictures into a scrapbook, is easier than sitting them down on the settee and formally going through your plans. Older children and teenagers will appreciate it if you tell them in such a way that invites their comments about the best way to approach the separation rather than making them feel that the changes that are coming are going to be forced upon them against their will. You may already have an idea about what the best arrangements for caring for your children are going to be, but that doesn't mean that this will automatically fit with what your children think is the best approach. When you talk to children about family separation give them a lot of time in which to ask you questions; do not, for example, talk to them half an hour before you are due to go out somewhere. Also, make sure that what you are telling them is unambiguous and truthful without going into too much detail.

Your children don't need to know the finer details of why the family is separating, but they do need to know the fact that you are going to be living differently. After you have talked about what is going to happen, make sure that you ask them to think about how they feel and if they have any worries or concerns to talk to you about. Be prepared for children to say nothing at all, teenagers might go off to their room for hours while young children might not appear to have understood. You can be sure that they will be processing the news, so do stay around the house and be available to reassure the children and talk to them about any worries they may have.

Consistency in arrangements

We cannot stress too strongly that consistency in arrangements, particularly in the early days of family separation, is a must for children. If you are unsure about when the actual separation is going to happen, forestall telling children until you know for sure. Do not, however, leave it until the last minute and announce the separation on the day the removal van pulls up outside your front door. Children need time to come to terms with what is going to happen, and they need to know that what you say will happen is what will actually happen. Right from day one of your family separating you should have arrangements in place for children to see both parents and/or talk to them at least once a day during the first weeks and then regularly throughout the week from then on. These arrangements should be consistent and should not be changed during the first months unless they really have to be. Your children need to know that they can still depend upon two parents and that those parents will always be there when they say they will be. Children respond well to consistent arrangements and can quickly regain the trust that they may have lost through the family separating when they know that they can continue to rely on their parents.

Giving reassurance

Children of all ages need reassurance but how you give that will differ depending upon their age. What you must never do is give children false reassurance, however distressed they are about mummy/daddy leaving home. Children need to hear that their other parent still loves them and will be there for them on a regular basis. Telling children that daddy will come back soon is not going to provide them with the inner reassurance that they need if it doesn't happen. Telling children that daddy still loves them and will talk to them on the phone tonight at 7.00 p.m. will start to rebuild their trust and confidence that, despite the change, their parents do still love them. Reassurance in the form of words backed up by actions is the only way to offer your children the ongoing security that they need. If you are due to phone at 7.00 p.m., make sure it is 7.00 p.m. and not ten past or quarter to seven when you do phone. If you are due to collect your children at 5.00 p.m., make sure you are there on the dot; if you are going to be late, telephone the other parent to inform them so that they can reassure the children that all is well. Nothing damages children more than an hour spent in the company of a frustrated parent who is angry that the other parent is not on time. Children become anxious and upset in these circumstances, worried about where the other parent is and whether they are going to turn up, and afraid that there will be an argument when they do. Parents who are waiting for the other parent to turn up must be on guard against showing their frustration in these circumstances. To prevent this, make sure that you agree that you will offer your children the reassurance of doing what you say you will do on time, and if you can't, commit to letting the other parent know ahead of time what is happening.

A charter for children living in separated family situations

This is not a legal charter but something that was suggested by two Family Court judges in America as a Bill of Rights. The charter relates to those things that parents most often do to their children during family separation. The charter is aimed at freeing children from the burdens placed upon them and, as such, forms a bill of responsibilities for parents to adhere to in order to protect their children from the worst effects of family separation. The provisions are:

1. Children have the right not to be asked to choose sides between their parents.

2. Children have the right not to be told the details of bitter or nasty legal proceedings going on between their parents.

3. Children have the right not to be told bad things about the other parent's personality or character.

4. Children have the right to privacy when talking to their other parent on the telephone.

5. Children have the right not to be interrogated or cross-examined after spending time with their other parent.

6. Children have the right not to be asked to tell untruths to their other parent.

7. Children have the right not to be used as confidants in regard to the legal proceedings between parents.

8. Children have the right not to be asked to be a messenger between one parent and the other.

9. Children have the right to express feelings whatever they may be.

10. Children have the right to choose not to express certain feelings.

11. Children have the right to be protected from parental warfare.

12. Children have the right not to be made to feel guilty for loving both parents.

Children's changing needs

What children need at the age of three is not going to be the same as what they need when they are 13. This is one of our main arguments against rigid shared-care arrangements. Children who are three years old need firm boundaries and complete consistency in arrangements. They respond well to these and can readily adapt to life in a separated family situation if two parents are able to share care in this way.

When children are older, however, they have more interests outside of the home and their friends start to become more important. It is when children reach this stage, with parties every Saturday and football on Sundays as well as after school activities, that greater flexibility is needed.

In many ways separated-parenting arrangements need to mirror the ways in which being a parent requires you to let your children go, a little bit at a time, so that they can learn independence and self-control. By the time your children reach adolescence they are likely to spend more of their time away from you and this can be tricky to arrange if you are intent on keeping the rigid shared-care arrangements in place.

As your children get older it is important that wherever they are, they can stay in touch with friends. Each parent needs to be prepared to do some of the ferrying around when the children are with them, and as children get older be prepared for fleeting glimpses of them as they arrive at your house only to disappear out of the door two minutes later to see friends. This is normal for children, and they need to be allowed to live their lives like this because it means that they are not having to negotiate their parent's needs, they are being allowed to fulfil their own.

By the time children get to around ten years of age they will want to be out with their friends more than spending time with you. Be prepared to facilitate this and also be flexible about arrangements. If your daughter is in one of those sleepover phases, every Saturday night is likely to be spent at someone else's house and every Sunday is likely to be spent with her moping around and falling asleep because she was up until 1.00 a.m. If you make sure that one of those Saturday nights is a sleepover at your house, you might see her for half an hour as she excitedly prepares the snacks and treats they are going to eat. The rest of the night is likely to be spent trying to get to sleep amidst the howls and screams of pre-pubescent girls terrifying themselves with ghost stories.

What we are saying here is that by the time children get to the age of ten or so, your parenting is about meeting their changing needs rather than meeting your own needs for time with them. This can be difficult to come to terms with if you have been sharing care; after all, you haven't seen them all week and as soon as they arrive they are off somewhere else again. Try to keep in mind that this is normal and that the task ahead of you now is to begin to allow your children appropriate levels of freedom and flexibility so that they can start to develop their independence and interest in the world outside of their life with parents.

Building flexibility into arrangements

It can be difficult to build flexibility into arrangements if you are the kind of person who likes to know what is happening and when. If you are easier going, flexibility won't be too difficult to establish. Ideally you will have agreed early on in your parenting arrangements that some flexibility is possible, particularly, for example, if children are ill or have important events in their lives such as weddings to attend.

The requirement for flexibility is something that you must deal with together. It is no good one parent being prepared to be flexible and the other being completely rigid in their approach. When we talk about flexibility, however, we are talking about being flexible in response to your children's needs not your own, although there should also be some room for agreed changes to arrangements so that illness and events in parents' lives are also taken into account.

Flexibility means being able to call the other parent and ask whether it is possible for you to drop the children off two hours later next week as they have been invited to a party. Flexibility means picking the children up yourself after the party so that the other parent doesn't have to. Flexibility means being able to ask the other parent if it's going to be OK for the children to stay an extra couple of nights this time as their cousins are visiting. Flexibility means saying that's not a problem and 'Why don't they stay with you for three extra nights and then I will pick them up at the weekend.'

Flexibility is not easy to achieve if you view your time with your children as being your 'right'. If you continue to do this as your children get older you will be in danger of asking your children to fulfil your needs rather than parenting them in ways that fulfils theirs.

Flexibility requires that you understand how your children need regular and consistent arrangements when they are younger and how this changes as they grow older. Flexibility to meet your children's changing needs is one of the key skills that good-enough parents possess. Good-enough separated parents take this skill and build it into their relationship with their children and their children's other parent.

Ensuring warmth and security in both homes

The ability to ensure your children are warm and secure in both homes is of the utmost importance, as the following study demonstrates.

Jack

A dad who had been sharing care of his children for some years told us one of the saddest stories we had ever heard. Jack had four children aged between nine and 15 and he had cared for them on a half-a-week basis for six years. He came to the Centre for Separated Families because he was struggling with his children, the eldest of whom was saying that she no longer wanted to live at his house. The reason why she didn't want to live there was because she didn't have a proper bedroom to herself, she had to share it with her sister, and also she didn't have a proper bed, she slept on a mattress on the floor.

Jack told us about the struggle that he had financially to keep caring for his children. He worked full-time in a factory and was not very well paid but he had managed to find himself a house to rent with enough space in it to have all of his children to live with him for half of the week. Unfortunately for Jack, he was not the parent with care as the children's mum claimed the child benefit and continued to do so when she left him to live with someone else. As this is lawful and the children were living with her for half the week, she assumed the role of parent with care and went on to claim child support.

Jack was paying his children's other parent around £90 per week in child support and, as a result, was finding things very difficult financially. While he had the bare basics for his children at home, there was no money spare to buy luxury items or things like new beds and bedding. In fact Jack was struggling so badly financially that he was existing on 9p tins of beans and a loaf of bread each week while his children were not with him, saving as much of his money as he could for the three nights each week they were living with him. As the children grew older and their mother's financial circumstances continued to improve after she remarried, they found themselves living fairly well for half of the week when they were with her and experiencing severe poverty for the other half when they were with their father.

By the time the eldest daughter was 15 she had her own room at her mother's house and was living a similar life to that of her friends. She no longer wanted to live at her father's home, however, simply because of his impoverished lifestyle. Jack told us that he didn't think he could go on caring for his children because he knew that they were suffering and were better off financially when they were with their mother. He was heartbroken and so were we because he had worked so hard to provide ongoing care for his children only to be defeated by circumstances.

If you are going to build a cooperative relationship we would urge you to keep this story in mind. We know that many children are at risk of poverty through living in separated family situations and that payment of child support is seen as being the answer to this problem. What we are saying is that the problem of poverty in separated families is not as cut and dried as some people would like us to believe. Separated parents find themselves in many different circumstances and it is important that you assess the overall ability of both of you to provide warm, safe and secure homes for your children if you are going to parent cooperatively. This might mean that you share the cost of important items, such as beds, from the outset and that you ensure together that your children's practical needs continue to be met throughout their lives.

Valuing and respecting the other parent

One parent valuing and respecting the other parent means that you continue to believe that they are important in your children's lives and ensuring that your children know that too. You do not have to like the other parent any longer but you do need to be prepared to respect their continued input into your children's lives and value the qualities that they bring to that. Children who know that their parents value and respect each other feel better about themselves and are free to live their lives without worrying about whether mum and dad are going to fall out again when it comes to parents' evening.

Knowing that parents may not like each other but that they do value each other means that children are enabled to value and respect all aspects of themselves, especially those that they identify as being similar to their parents.

Valuing and respecting the other parent means being committed to talking respectfully about them and not undermining them in front of your children. If you disagree with something that the other parent has told a child it may be important to say so, but it is important that you do so in a way that does not denigrate the parent. Saying, 'Well I don't think I agree with what your dad has said but I will chat to him about it later' gives a very different message to children than if you say, 'Your father never ever gets things right and here he is again getting it wrong, I am going to tell him how useless he is.'

Helping teenagers to take control of the arrangements

At some point in your children's lives they will be ready to take more control over the arrangements for where they live. When they reach this point you must try to allow them the right to make their own decisions, even if they decide that they just want to live in one place. Moving from one house to another can get complicated for teenagers, who can start to feel that they just want to be in one place from where they can go off and explore the world. Other teenagers might feel that they want the reassurance of continuing with arrangements just as they are. If your teenager seems to be finding things difficult, try to find some time together so that they can talk if they want to. Introducing the subject by saying something along the lines of 'How are you finding the arrangements between me and your dad these days?' is useful, but be prepared for the truth and that the truth might not be something that you want to hear.

Ideally, by the time your children have reached the age of 13 there will be some flexibility in your arrangements, with the children themselves setting the pace and making the changes that they want to see. In our experience, teenagers who have lived in separated families where their needs come first do not suddenly decide that they want to change things. Some minor changes might happen such as staying over at friends' houses or needing to change arrangements because of part-time jobs, but, on the whole, teenagers who have been listened to throughout their lives will be able to ask for what they need.

Teenagers become problematic if the arrangements are too

rigid and if parents are not willing to be flexible. Providing that teenagers can feel that they will be listened to and that their reasonable requests for change will be met, there are likely to be few problems.

A WORD OF CAUTION

We would sound a word of caution here and that is that teenagers who live in separated family situations, where they are moving from one house to another on a regular basis, are definitely in need of continued parental guidance and supervision. If parents slacken the reins too quickly there is a risk of missing the signs that teenagers are involved in risky behaviour. Leaving one home in the morning for school and then arriving at the other parent's home in the evening means that some important issues might get overlooked. We are not saying that all teenagers will indulge in risky behaviour as soon as they are out of the sight of their parents; we are saying there is a risk it might be missed in the transition from one home to the other. A high level of parental communication is still as important when parenting teenagers separately, in fact it is probably more important than when children are younger. Regular time to talk to the other parent about how the teenager is performing at school, who the teenager is friends with and so on is vitally important. Your teenager needs to feel flexibility but also needs to know that the two of you are continuing to supervise and guide them through to adulthood.

Conclusion

Parenting after family separation does not have to be the conflict-ridden experience that many people struggle with.

Parenting well after family separation can be easy if you are prepared to follow some simple rules, such as keeping new partners out of the picture and continuing to value and respect your children's other parent.

Consistency and reliability

At all ages children thrive if their separated parents can continue to demonstrate that they will put their needs first. Consistency and reliability are the key words for younger children, and flexibility and guidance are the key words for parenting older children.

Children go through similar emotional processes as their parents when the family separates and these might not always be easy to spot. Learning about how children react at different ages can offer you the knowledge and skills to meet your children's changing needs.

Not every child who experiences family separation will go on to have difficulty in their own adult relationships. Family separation does not need to have the profoundly negative impact that many people assume it will.

Conflict is the key area that has a negative impact on children and it is the level and length of exposure to this that is deeply damaging.

Finally, children can and do thrive in separated families and can easily adapt to living for some of the week in one home and the rest in another. Ensuring their warmth and safety in both homes is imperative, as is establishing continuity and consistency in your arrangements. Keep in mind that your children have the right to a relationship with all of the significant people in their lives after family separation, and that it is your responsibility as parents to help them achieve this. Value and respect all of the people in your children's families of origin and you will help them to build self-respect and self-worth that will last them for the rest of their lives.

Personal Story
Annie, aged 25 – mum to Ollie and Keane – twins aged three

I don't know whether my story is unusual but I have two boys aged three, and I separated from their dad before they were born. We weren't married and had only been together for about 18 months when I found out I was pregnant. We lived in Cornwall at the time; I worked in a surf shop in Newquay and Ben, their dad, worked as a surf-school instructor. We spent loads of time together and were really happy until I found out I was pregnant.

When I told Ben that I was pregnant he was shocked and also horrified, I think. I was only 21 at the time and he was only 22. He didn't want me to have the baby but tried his best to be supportive while I decided what to do. We didn't even live together and I didn't have a flat, although he did. I lived in a shared house in Newquay and that was never going to be a suitable place to have children.

After a week or so of agonising I decided that I wanted to have the baby, and that I would bring it up on my own if Ben didn't want to be involved. I don't think that Ben was very happy about it but he said he would do every-thing he could to support me and stay with me. I suppose that the problem was that we were really young and our relationship was just a bit of fun, like it is, I suppose, when you are in your early twenties. The other thing was that Ben was planning to go to art school in Devon in the September of the following year, which would be two months after the birth; he had been offered a place that year but had deferred it so that he could spend the year with me.

After a month or so I moved into the flat with Ben and we started to get some things for the baby when it came. I kept on working at the shop but by then it was the middle of winter and my hours were cut. Of course Ben had finished at the surf school until the following spring and so he got a job in Falmouth on the boats. That meant he was up and out by 6.00 a.m. and not home until gone 7.00 p.m. I spent a lot of time on my own and got a bit fed up really I suppose. I was crabby when he got in and we were always arguing; it wasn't a very nice feeling, it was as though I had forced him into the situation and I got a bit tired of being stuck inside all of the time.

When I was four months pregnant I went for a scan and they told us it was twins. I just cried and cried for about 24 hours, it felt like my whole world had come crashing down on me. I couldn't think how we would manage with two children, we could barely work out how to manage one between us. Because it was twins I got very big by six months and had to go into hospital to rest during the last three months. That made things very bad for both of us because Ben was free to do as he pleased and I was just stuck there all day every day. Ben did come and see me but gradually it came down to him popping in now and then and us arguing every time he did. By the time it got to me being full-term we had just drifted apart I suppose, and we agreed that we should split up.

That left me in an almost impossible position. I had nowhere to live and I was going to have twins in a couple of weeks. I was desperate and didn't know which way to turn but the midwives and the social workers at the hospital in Truro were brilliant. I was assessed for a local authority house immediately and I even got the keys while I was still in hospital. Ben helped to shift my stuff over and painted the place for me. He made the nursery look beautiful, and my aunt gave me £500 to buy furniture and things like a fridge and a cooker.

I had the boys by Caesarean section on 30 July; it was such a hot day that there were fans in the operating theatre and all the nurses were sweating. The birth was fine and Ben was with me; he held Keane first and showed him to me and then Ollie came out and he showed him to me too and I held him. I didn't feel weepy or anything, I was a bit frightened by the anaesthetic, but apart from that I was totally fine. Ben was a bit emotional and spent a long time just sitting with both boys on his lap.

After I came home from hospital we had to start to work out how to be mum and dad to the boys if we were not going to be together. During the first weeks Ben stayed with me and helped me to feed them and change them day and night. I was breastfeeding but also bottle-feeding so that made it easier. Ben would get up and start the feeds at night and I would get up and finish them. Sometimes we were feeding from 2.00 a.m. until about 5.00 a.m. with both boys needing changing and then feeding again until they were ready to go back to sleep. It was really important for me to have Ben there, and if we hadn't been able to sort that out I think it would have been a massive opportunity missed for Ben to get to know his sons properly.

Ben went off to college in early October but came back every weekend until the boys got to be about two years old. That year was Ben's final year at college, though, and so we saw less of him as time went on. It was quite difficult at times that year because Ben was having a relationship with a girl at college which meant that he wasn't really interested in seeing the boys so much. I got quite angry with him because he was letting this thing with this girl get in the way of his relationship with his sons.

During this last year we have tried to formalise the arrangements between us and organise regular time for the boys to be with Ben. We got some help with doing that because we had got to the point where we couldn't talk at all about things. Ben couldn't see why there needed to be regular arrangements, but I knew that the boys needed to know when they were going to see him and that not seeing him, or him promising to come and not turning up, was having a bad effect on them.

Now they see Ben every two weeks from Friday night until Sunday night and during the other week he picks them up from nursery at 3.00 p.m. and takes them home to his flat for tea; if the weather is good they go pretend surfing. Ben has bought them both wetsuits and they look adorable in them with their blond curly hair and podgy little tummies. I think Ben realises how important it is for them to know when they are going to see him. We bought two calendars, one for our house and one for Ben's flat, and every month we mark down on each one the days that they will be with Ben. They are always really excited when it's time to go to his house for the weekend; I'm sure that's because they get spoiled rotten by Ben and his mum, who always calls down to see them on Sunday lunchtime. When it's the weekend when Ben has them I make sure to do something a bit wild for myself.

I'm still only 25 and it's very, very hard work having two boys aged three. I just thank goodness that I am young and fit because they can be exhausting. Anyway, I go a bit wild at the weekend and then I am calm and sensible again. I want to be the best mum I can be to them and I don't think it's a good idea for me to be going wild and then not being able to get up in the morning. Eventually I would like to meet someone and have a long-term relationship. It would have to be someone special, though, because my boys come first. So whoever I meet in the future will need to understand that and have a lot of energy and enthusiasm too because twin boys are a real handful!

Chapter 4

You and Your Children

'When my partner announced that she was going to leave me, I was devastated. It came as a complete shock. What was even worse was that she said that she was taking our two children with her. I thought that I would never get over the pain of that. I mean, I'd been involved in every part of their lives, you know – a real hands-on dad for four years. But we organised things so that they lived with me for three days a week and I built a new kind of life with them. Now, after 12 years, I wonder whether I've actually got more out of being a dad to them than if their mum hadn't left me. It's been fantastic!'
Ben – father of two

WHATEVER THE CIRCUMSTANCES that lay behind your family separation, regardless of whether you feel as though you were wronged, irrespective of whether you and the other parent agreed that there should be a separation or not, your relationship with your child or children will change and will change for ever.

This may feel terrifying but the change need not be for the worse. It is possible to have an even stronger and more fulfilling parenting relationship with your children. But, in order to achieve this, you need to be able and willing to put

135

the work in. You will need to understand what is happening to you and to your relationship with the other parent and what your children will be experiencing in order to make the changes successfully. The previous chapters will help you in this.

Making your children feel secure

Family separation is, usually, an extremely distressing experience for parents. They will be losing so many things that they have invested their lives in and the future may well look very uncertain. Adjustment to new ways of living, having to deal with the practicalities of separating and trying to find a new way of living can be both a bewildering and frightening process.

Imagine what this must feel like for your children. Not only do they have to negotiate the changes that they are presented with but they have no real power with which to influence them. All that once seemed safe and certain is thrown up in the air and they must come to terms with a world that will look very different from the one that they have grown up with. It is your job, as a parent, to make sure that you do everything in your power to help them make the transitions that will be necessary.

Remaining an adult

The most important task that you will face is ensuring that you remain an adult in your relationship with your child or children. This may seem like an odd thing to say because clearly you *are* an adult and your children *are* children. But the old parent–child relationship has been disrupted and it is your job to create a new one that allows your children to stay as children and does not require them to assume any of the responsibilities of adulthood.

Family separation is very often a distressing time for all those involved and, in this upheaval, children may experience all kinds of emotional struggles that can lead to them stepping out of their childhood and attempting to take on the emotional work of their parents.

When children see their parents in distress, they will very often try to find ways to make them feel better. Without proper care and attention, this can lead to an ongoing situation where the child is taking on the role of the adult while the parent adopts the role of the child.

In other situations, particularly where there is only one child or where one child is significantly older than their siblings, a child may take on the role of a missing parent.

You must be aware all of the time that you are not requiring your children to grow up too quickly, to be involved in things that really only properly concern adults or that you are allowing them to do the emotional work for you that you should really be doing for them.

If you want your children to grow up feeling safe, secure and loved, make sure that you are the adult and allow them to continue to experience their lives in a way that is appropriate to their age. The following example shows the issues that can arise.

Richard

Three months ago Richard's wife left him, and his two young daughters, Sam and Sue, live with him every weekend. One evening, Richard is overcome with sadness and begins to cry. Seeing this, Sam gets up from playing with her younger sister and puts her arm around her father's shoulders, reassuring him that everything is going to be OK. She then makes her father a cup of tea and they spend the rest of the evening watching television together.

Because Richard is so happy and proud that his daughter is such a caring child and because the incident seems to suggest to him that his children really do want to be with him every weekend (he had feared that they would really rather be with his ex-wife and her new partner in the family home), both children are allowed to stay up for an extra hour.

In many ways, this is a rather touching example in that it describes a closeness between a father and his two daughters after family separation. Sam displays a highly developed sense of emotional maturity and there would seem to be a good chance that this family unit will last.

Underneath this, though, lies a problem with the boundaries between the responsibilities that Richard, as an adult, has and the responsibilities that Sam, as a child, has taken upon herself.

If Sam and Sue are to grow into emotionally strong and secure adults, then their parents need to be sure not to burden them inadvertently with their own emotional needs.

It is not Sam's responsibility to make Richard feel better about what has happened to the family, it is his responsibility to take control of all the emotional danger and process it on behalf of his children.

It would have been far better if Richard had acknowledged his daughter's concern but demonstrated to her that he was capable of dealing with his sadness himself and then offered to make his children a drink. It would also have been better not to have extended bedtime as this reinforces the idea in his daughter's head that the emotional responses that they are processing have an effect on the structure of their lives.

Reassure your children

One of the most important things that parents provide for their children is reassurance. Adults should be there to protect children from all of the things that scare them or make them feel in any way insecure. And there are few things scarier than the domestic world you have grown up with being shattered – even if that life had been far from ideal.

That isn't to say that you should pretend that things don't hurt or deny your children the opportunity to feel and express their anxiety. Pretending that nothing has changed and that everything is fine can be just as damaging for children because it runs contrary to their experience.

What it does mean is that parents need to acknowledge their children's anxieties and some of their own emotional hurt but that they make it clear that they can and will deal with them.

If your child came in from playing outside crying because they had hurt their leg, you wouldn't think of saying, 'But I've just trapped my finger in the door and I need you to put a plaster on me.' You would deal with your child's need for care and reassurance. Then, perhaps, you might tell your child about what you had just done but you would find a plaster for yourself!

In the same way, while you may be torn apart inside, deal with your children's needs in a way that makes them feel safe and deal with your own hurt away from them. Use Chapter 1 of this book to help you better understand the feelings that you are likely to be experiencing and ideas about ways to deal with them.

You may want to cry and shout and smash things up, but you must find the courage to continue to be an adult *and* to be a parent to your child or children. Never let your emotional needs take precedence over theirs and never ask *them* to make *you* feel safe.

Don't require your children to look after you

The insecurity that often accompanies a traumatic event like family separation can mean that we seek love and comfort from those around us in order to reassure us that we are 'good' people. The rejection of our love by someone in whom we placed our trust can be an extremely wounding experience, and so it is understandable that we may look to our children to confirm to us that we are still worthy of love.

Whereas there is no harm in us basking in the warmth of the positive reflections we receive from our children, it is positively harmful for us to require our children to look after our emotional needs. Although we may experience a degree of strength from the reflection of ourselves that our children give us, it is our responsibility as adults to provide our children with love and emotional security, not the other way round.

Children will, very often, pick up on our emotional vulnerability and feel that they have a duty to make us 'feel better'. Do not, on any account, allow this to become a dynamic between yourself and your child or children. As soon as you feel that it may be happening – regardless of how miserable you may be feeling – drag yourself up by the scruff of the neck and make sure that you make them feel loved and secure, because underneath their desire to make you feel better is a fear and insecurity that is your job to deal with.

New patterns of parenting

The establishment of new patterns of parenting can be one of the most fraught and potentially conflictual points between you and the other parent. This is an area that we deal with more fully in Chapter 6. However, it is important to recognise at this stage how the pattern of parenting that you end up with will affect the choices you make.

Each set of circumstances will vary according to the history of the family, the reason for separation, the nature of the relationship with the other parent and a whole host of other variables. You may find yourself caring for your children on a full-time or near full-time basis. You may work out a half-time caring arrangement after separation. You may see your children only at weekends or only in the school holidays.

Many parents find themselves in situations of extremely damaging conflict over the amount of caring time that they will each provide for their children. Sometimes it is because one parent feels that they are not getting enough, and sometimes it is because one parent feels that the other is not prepared to provide enough hands-on parenting. Either way, you must both put the needs of your children first and not use the division of parenting time as a weapon with which to beat the other parent.

Make the arrangements work

At the Centre for Separated Families, we made a huge cultural change in our work by recognising, validating and supporting both parents after separation. We believe that, at the time of making this change, it was unique among family support services in the UK, either state or voluntary provided.

The reason that we did this was because we recognised that the parent that provided, or was granted, the least amount of parenting time was unsupported and, as a result, children risked the loss of this parent's input.

We believe, and our work with children and research into separated families has shown, that children almost always value the parenting input of both parents, even where that might be small or imperfect. And, because children value it, we value it.

Whether you feel that you have been allowed the parenting input that you desired or whether you feel unjustly treated, you have a responsibility to try to make the arrangements work for your children. It is their needs as children that should take precedence over your needs as adults.

By all means, try to find remedies if you feel that you have been treated unjustly, but deal with your hurt or anger away from your children and, most importantly, make sure that you do what you say you will do. Never be tempted to frustrate the other parent's parenting time in order to score points or exercise power over the other parent. You may well produce the intended reaction but you will also harm your children in the process. They are not a part of any conflict between you and their other parent and you should not want them to be.

It is quality not quantity that counts

Don't imagine that any one pattern of parenting after separation is necessarily better than any other. What we have found to be the most important to children is not the type, pattern or quantity of parenting but its certainty, regularity and quality.

Whatever pattern of parenting time you and the other parent adopt, make sure that your children know what it is and make sure that you stick to it. If either of you need to vary it at any time, make sure that your children know about it in advance. The arrangements that you have made, whether you are happy with them or not, are not just arrangements between you and the other parent, they are a compact, a promise, to your children and they will feel hurt and let down if you do not honour it.

Don't think that because you may only have limited parenting time that this is in any way less important to your children. What is important is how they experience that time, and that is something that you have a huge degree of control over. We find that, even if a child is only with one parent for a few hours a week, if that time is a happy one, and they know it will be there come rain or shine, it can provide a real sense of ongoing care and reassurance.

So, if pick-up time is one o'clock, make sure you are there at one o'clock. You will be surprised at not only how much children value this but also how much they measure their own sense of importance by it. In other words, if you can't be bothered to arrive when you have said you will, children will very often interpret this to mean that they are not very important to you.

Your new parenting situation

When your family separates, it is almost certain that your children will experience your actions in one of four ways:

- You will have left their other parent and taken them with you.

- You will have left their other parent and not taken them with you.

- You and your children will have been left by the other parent.

- The other parent will have left you and taken the children with them.

Each of these different situations will always have an impact on the nature of the relationship between yourself and your children in the future.

This is because your child or children will not only experience your physical presence in a different way (if you have taken the children with you or have been left with the children then you are likely to have to provide more day-to-day care) but, to a degree, they will also experience and empathise with you and the situation you find yourself in.

It is not uncommon for children to feel sorry for one parent or to withdraw from the other. They may find that they are angry with you for having left them or for having taken them away from their other parent. They may be angry with you for forcing their other parent to leave the family home or for taking them to a new home that is away from their friends.

They may feel sad for you because they see you in a new flat that is badly furnished. They may feel sad for you because you are all alone in the old family home where once their toys and clothes were but now there are only empty spaces.

They may need to adjust to the fact that whereas prior to the separation you were the parent who came in late after work and spent the weekend volunteering as a potholing club leader, they are now expected to spend one full night during the week and all day Sunday watching DVDs with you and going for walks and painting and playing on the games console and a thousand other activities that you seem to have decided you should all be doing together!

They may resent the fact that whereas you were once a constant fixture in their lives, they now have to spend several days a week away from you and wonder what they have done to deserve it.

In our experience, there is not one set of problems that is going to fit each category and each child will experience and react to the parenting environment in his or her own individual way. What is important is that you are prepared for the fact that there will need to be a period of adjustment and that it is your job to ensure that your child or children remain safe and secure through that process.

Chapter 3 looks in detail at the ways in which children may react to their changed circumstances. Even where things appear to be progressing fairly smoothly, it is necessary to understand the potential effects on your children that family separation may bring about. This is because many children, for fear of making you more unhappy than you already appear to be, can become very effective at hiding the emotional anxieties that they may be experiencing.

Talking with your children

In order to help your child or children to make the transition from a family that lives together to one where they are parented separately by mum and dad, it is important that you help them to understand and be able to talk about what is happening to them and, also, what is happening to you as their parents.

Talking in this way with your children may be something that is new to you and it may be something that you feel uncomfortable about doing. It may be something that you need to learn for yourself, but you will be doing your children a great service if you are able to do so in a way that is clear and appropriate.

The first step is to recognise and name what is happening around your child or children. Whereas it is always necessary to think about what information is suitable never be tempted to lie or tell half-truths. Truth is invariably less damaging than fiction.

Always acknowledge that both you and the other parent still love your child or children. This can be a very, very difficult thing to do especially if you have been hurt by the other parent's actions or where the other parent has simply walked away from you and the children. Nevertheless, it is important that you say this to your children, whatever the circumstances. Not to do so runs the risk of seriously damaging their sense of security and emotional well-being in the world.

Listen to your children's experiences

Never try to brush your children's experience of the separation under the carpet. Offering comforting words while not allowing your children to express their feelings will delay or prevent them from coming to terms with the changes that are going on around them.

Talking with your children about what is happening can be very difficult because, not only does it bring up all the painful things that you may have been trying to deal with yourself as a result of the separation, it also means that you have to hear and deal with the hurt that it has brought to your children.

Allowing your children to express their fears and anxieties, though, will help them adjust to the new situation and, in the long term, will mean that old painful feelings will be less likely to resurface in later childhood or adulthood.

It may be that you are still so emotionally hurt and enmeshed in what has happened to you that you simply can't talk to your children in any way that will help them; indeed, it could make things worse. If you believe that this is the case, consider whether it may be possible for someone else to take on this role until you are in a better and stronger emotional state yourself. This could be a relative, a friend who has a strong relationship with your children or even a professional, such as a teacher or carer. Don't forget, though, that there is no real substitute for you as a parent, so get working on processing your emotional hurts and fears and then help your children with theirs.

Men can talk too

The task of talking to their children about feelings may be particularly difficult for men. This is because men tend to be socialised into not discussing emotions and not showing or admitting to weaknesses. It is important to understand that the suppression of emotional anguish can be very harmful both psychologically and physically. (Chapter 1 deals with this in some detail.) Learning to be open about how you feel and being able to respond to your child's emotional needs can be a very important step forward, therefore, both as a man and as a parent. However, you may find that you need to talk to someone you trust beforehand, in order to hear yourself expressing your feelings out loud.

Tell your children what is happening

It is important that your children know what is happening and why their parents are separating. Keeping them in the dark only adds to their sense of unease and insecurity.

Ensure that they know the real reason why you are separating. If you say nothing then children may draw their own conclusions that will very often put themselves at the centre, or even the cause, of the problems. Equally, lies and half-truths are usually exposed at some point which means that sooner or later your children are going to have to deal with what really happened. This may be many years down the line when they have felt that they had dealt with all they needed to and had adjusted to the separation – not an ideal situation.

147

When considering what and how to tell your child or chil-dren about the separation, make sure that it is age and experience appropriate. What and how you tell a 13-year-old will not be the same as what and how you tell a six-year-old.

Don't ask your children to share your anger

Very importantly, avoid blaming or rubbishing the other parent. It may well be true that the other parent is a good-for-nothing waster who cares more about horse racing than he does about you. All your children need to know is that their father liked to spend a lot of time and money on horse racing and that you wanted a life that didn't involve that. You might want to explain the effect that this had on you but make sure that this is at an appropriate level. Don't forget that whatever you might think about the other parent, to your children he is just dad and they may well feel protective of him.

Equally, the other parent may have fallen in love with your best friend, but you need present this only as a fact to your children. It is not necessary for you to question her morality or integrity or go into great details about how and when she had betrayed you. She is, after all, their mum and they still love her.

It may be that, as the years progress, your children may want to know more about the circumstances that brought about the family separation and, as they get older, you may decide that it is appropriate to talk in more detail about what happened. Always remember, though, that the reason for discussing the events is to help your children understand better what happened and not an excuse for you to exact revenge. Apart from anything else, it usually backfires!

Your own sense of hurt can harm your children

Expecting your children to share your anger about the other parent can backfire in two ways. First, there is a good chance that they will simply rally to defend the other parent, and so the more hostility you display the more they will feel the need to support the other parent – quite often at your expense.

Even if you succeed in winning your children round to your point of view, you may very well still harm their chances of growing into assured and emotionally rounded adults capable of forming their own loving relationships in the future.

We worked with a man whose mother left his father to care for him alone in his early teenage years. We had no way of really knowing the truth behind the separation, but the family myth that the father had succeeded in having accepted was that the mother, in keeping with all women, was selfish, untrustworthy and promiscuous. So well re-inforced was this family myth that the man who came to seek our help was incapable of forming trusting relationships with women and was always looking for them to harm him.

Had the father been able to deal with his own anger and hurt away from the boy then it may have been possible for the actions and the decisions of the parents not to come back to haunt the son in his adult life. Indeed, not only the son, but *his* children too, because this millstone had meant that his own adult parenting relationship had suffered.

Children need to be told that they aren't responsible

As we have discussed, children very often believe that they have, in some way, been responsible for their parent's separation. You must make sure that you reassure them about this and explain to them that a sense of guilt and responsibility is a common and natural response to feelings of loss and grief.

It is also very important that children understand that they cannot and are not expected to bring separated parents back together again. Very often, children will fantasise about their parents coming back together and assume the responsibility of mediating this. They need to understand that this will not happen.

Take the lead in expressing your feelings

Children will often not know what is OK for them to say about how they feel. They seek to protect you from their anguish as they think that this will make it more painful for you and more unsafe for them.

You can help them express their emotions by taking a lead. Try saying things like 'You seem sad today' or 'I can understand why you might feel angry.' You can also model, for children, the expression of feeling by using phrases like 'Sometimes, I'm so angry I could scream.' In doing this, you may well reflect your child's feelings in a way that makes it all right for them to say it or gives them permission to express a different feeling but in a similar way.

Tears do help

Don't try to stop children from expressing their sadness through tears. Crying is a very natural way for children and adults, too, to express and release feelings of sadness, anger and hurt.

It is important that you allow children and young adults of all ages to cry if that is what they need to do. Don't try to stop them because it pains you to see their sadness or because you feel that the tears represent continued pain (the tears are actually part of the healing process) or because you feel that it is inappropriate for children of a certain age or gender to express their feelings through crying.

Boys may well find it difficult to show what they are really feeling or allow themselves to cry because many will have been taught that crying is a sign of weakness. Fathers, in particular, can really help their sons by allowing them to cry. It isn't soft or unmanly; it is a healthy and natural expression of feeling.

Creating new routines for your children

We have found that one of the most important things in making the transition from a family that lives together to one that lives apart as uncomplicated and secure for children as possible is the establishment of routine.

Children, especially younger ones, thrive on routine. It puts the world into order for them and places secure boundaries between themselves and a world of freedom and responsibility that they are not yet ready to encounter.

From a very young age, babies and toddlers find security and peace in routine. Whether that is a bedtime routine of tea, bath, story and bed by six o'clock or some other regular pattern that they encounter day by day, it means that they don't need to be responsible for the external world. They are too young and haven't learned, yet, to set their own boundaries, and so the creation and maintenance of such boundaries by parents and other adults gives children the security that they need to continue to be children.

Family separation can bring with it a huge range of emotional anxieties for children and, if old routines and boundaries are not maintained or new ones are not established, it can feel to them as if the whole world is in total chaos. This not only makes them feel unsafe in the world but also forces them into a position where they, themselves, need to try to make sense of the external world, which is something that they should not be required, and are not equipped, to do.

Again, these boundaries and routines are ones that you need to set for yourself – hopefully in agreement with the other parent. They should be based on past patterns but also take account of the new circumstances.

If you feel that you and the other parent had not set or stuck to proper routines while you were together, now could be a good time to start afresh. As long as boundaries are well considered and age appropriate, even a bit of initial grumbling shouldn't last very long.

You may find that with older children it is helpful to talk about the boundaries and routines that you think are appropriate and have a discussion about what is and what is not reasonable.

Our experience is that chaos is never helpful! You, as an adult, need to be strong enough to provide the boundaries that your children need and not to let any sense of hopelessness that you may feel get in the way of creating a new ordered and settled environment for your children.

Tips on establishing new routines

Here are a few examples of the kinds of routines that you may find helpful as you begin to create and establish your own. If you already have this in hand, feel free to skip this section.

You will need to think about routines in two ways – the routine into which your parenting time will fit and the routines that will exist within that parenting time.

- Try to reach an agreement with the other parent about when each of you will be parenting your child or children. It may be that you agree to share that responsibility half and half or it may be that one of you is able or more willing to provide a greater share of the hands-on care.

- Whatever agreement you come to or whatever parenting time you are seeking, make sure that your primary concern is the happiness and well-being of your children. Try to think about what they might be comfortable with. It may be helpful to look at the patterns of parenting before the separation, or where one parent has walked away from their parenting responsibilities, you may try to ask that partner to reflect on how that will feel to the child or children.

- Wherever possible, try to establish a routine as soon as you can so that your child or children can deal with their feelings about the separation within a structured external world.

- If the children will live with one parent on two days a week, it can be useful to establish which days these will be. Very quickly, children will adapt to this and know that Thursday is swimming lessons and then dad picks us up.

- If you only see your children for a few hours at the weekend, try to make that the same few hours each time. Your children can then put other things into order around this. Things like watching their favourite television programmes or letting their friends know when they will be around to play. You may want to talk to them in advance of setting the routine so as not to interfere with something that is important to them. After all, you don't want your three hours on a Saturday afternoon to prevent your daughter from meeting her friends in town and she may not feel able to tell you this. Far better to find a time that suits her so that the hours that you spend together are free and easy.

- It is important to stress, again, the need to stick to the arrangements you have made. If you see your children for three hours on Sunday morning, make sure that not only are you where you say you will be but that you are in a fit state to make that time worthwhile for your children. In other words, you may need to make Friday night your night out rather than Saturday – you can't expect your children to be the only ones required to change their lifestyles.

- Equally, it is important that *both* parents make the new arrangements work. If the arrangement is that your child's father will see your son on a Saturday night, you need to honour this even if your friend has asked you to stay over and you can't face driving into town and back.

Be prepared to be flexible

Even where there is routine, there needs to be flexibility. Having established a clear structure for your children, don't make it so rigid that there is no room for flexibility or spontaneity. Don't prevent your children from attending a sleepover just because it is 'your night to have them'. Discuss it with the other parent and see if you and the children might spend some other time together or whether, if sleepovers are becoming a common occurrence, it might be better to change the night that they stay with you.

By the same token, be prepared to allow your children the opportunity to spend a little longer with the other parent if this will facilitate an experience that they will enjoy or benefit from. For example, if it is not possible for the other parent to take your child to a football match because the agreement is that their parenting time is on a Saturday morning, consider agreeing a change or extension to the time. This will allow your child to go to the match, show your child that you and the other parent are capable of compromise and will have the added benefit of reducing conflict between yourself and the other parent.

Not everything needs to change

Don't change routines just for the sake of it. If you are providing most of the hands-on parenting, it can be a good thing to keep as many things the same as they have always been, particularly in the early weeks and months after separation. This stability of routine can act as a counterbalance to the other changes that are going on in your children's lives.

You may wish to remove all traces of the other parent from your home; but consider how this might feel for your children. Also, think about ways in which it may be possible to combine your need to clear the other parent out of your life and house with their need to still have two parents. With a bit of thought and, with older children, discussion it can be possible.

You may find that it is difficult to go to the same places that you and the other parent used to go to – even shops and cafés can bring up painful memories – but try to balance your potential for experiencing pain against your children's need for continuity. Again, with care and attention, this can be possible.

It can be a good idea to think about the routines that you

and your children have already established and think about which ones you want to maintain and which ones you want to change.

Change can also be a positive thing

Change can be a healthy and positive thing for children of all ages, although you need to ensure that any change is structured and not chaotic. Children will be far happier with a change that becomes predictable – for example, that every Tuesday night you all go to the cinema – rather than unpredictable – for example, that they go to bed at a different time each night or that you constantly take them over to see your friends at short notice.

Having considered the routines that you have found useful in the past and wish to continue with (a regular bedtime is a good example of this), you may decide to introduce new routines. This can be especially helpful if your relationship with the other parent has descended into chaotic behaviour or inertia prior to the final separation.

You may wish to introduce regular mealtimes if they did not previously exist, a regular trip to the library or to a grandparent's house can be enjoyable for both you and your child. If you are providing most of the hands-on parenting, it will give you a rest and a chance to recuperate if you allow your children to attend clubs or visit relatives on a regular day. Not only will they get a great deal out of it but it will provide you with regular and predictable space to relax or catch up on things that need attending to.

Predictability can provide a framework, especially in the time immediately after a separation, in which both adults and children can begin to come to terms with what has happened. Routine can place a protective arm around your external lives when your emotional world is in chaos.

Younger children, in particular, will find security in regularity; just as in the same way that they ask for the same story to be read to them over and over again, so they find comfort in knowing that each day will have a certainty that tells them that everything is in its place.

Carving out new routines away from the family home

Some separating parents make an arrangement known as 'nesting', whereby the children remain in the family home at all times and the parents move in and out (see Chapter 6). This is an unusual arrangement but, if done carefully and thoughtfully, it can be a very useful model of post-separation parenting as the children experience a great deal of continuity and security.

Usually, however, leaving the family home will be experienced by one if not both parents after separation. This can be very stressful and, if your children will be staying in your new home, it is important to make this a familiar and emotionally safe environment as soon as possible.

This will depend entirely on the pattern and circumstances of your parenting. How you do it if your children live with you for four three or four nights a week may be very different from how you approach things if your children are only with you during the school holidays.

It can often be comforting for children, especially younger ones, to have familiar things in this new space, but be careful. Don't insist that half of your children's belongings are moved to the new house. Your children may prefer to keep most of their things in one place but may well be happy to bring a few treasured items (such as teddies) with them. Let your children take the lead on this. It may be that you can make a special place for teddy to sit when he comes to visit with your child and that he is welcomed into the new home as much as the little person who brings him!

Let your children see that you are a capable adult in this new space and offer it to them to share. If they will be spending time there on a weekly basis, consider deciding on how it might look, together. For instance, children love to help with the decorating and arrangement of furniture and it will help them feel as though they have a place and a stake in this new home.

If your children live with you only in the school holidays, be prepared for their arrival. Give them a description of the place and the surrounding area that they will be visiting. Organise some things that you could do during their stay with you but be prepared for them to want to do something different or, perhaps, nothing at all. Try not to see a rejection of your plans as a rejection of you – don't overindulge your children but don't demand too much from them either. You may be able to provide your children with some wonderful childhood memories that they will carry with them into adulthood, but this won't happen if you are trying to fit square pegs into round holes.

If your children are living with you on a more regular basis then the routines that you establish may be more everyday things, but they will help to make your new home their home too. Find places for them to put their shoes, make a space for them to have a few books, buy some plates and cutlery together and agree who will do the washing-up and who will empty the rubbish.

There are a number of tasks that dads, in particular, may not have carried out when the family was living together. If this is the case then you will need to get to grips with these as soon as possible. Little things can make life so much easier for both yourself and your children; things like ensuring that their clothes are clean and put out for them in the morning ready for school or that there are enough cornflakes for when they arrive.

Creating routine without a new home

It is not uncommon for a parent who leaves the family home to move into accommodation that is not suitable for children to visit or stay at. You may, for example, find yourself sleeping on the settee at a friend's flat or in a homeless hostel. This isn't only very depressing in itself but can make it even more difficult to forge a new way of being with your children following the family separation.

Regardless of how difficult this may be, it is vital that you continue to make the effort. As long as you are continuing to provide them with safe and positive parenting, your children will benefit greatly from your continued input. It may not be the way that you want to parent but, from your children's point of view, you are still a person that they love and need; make it as positive as you can for them.

If you can afford to eat out or go to the cinema together, then this can be part of a new routine. But if money is tight, there are still plenty of things that you can do, such as going for walks together, visiting the public library or the park. Don't dismiss ordinary things, like sharing a family meal at a child's grandparents' house, as these types of activity can be very enjoyable experiences for children and reassure them that there is some continuity in their lives.

Hopefully, your current situation will be a temporary one and it is important that you continue to be present for your children even if it is only for a few hours each week or fortnight because it can be more problematic to try to establish a new parenting relationship with your child or children some months down the line.

Helping your children to have two homes

When we give lectures and presentations around family separation and the possibilities and pitfalls of shared care arrangements, one of the questions that comes up over and over again is around children having to negotiate the physical and emotional move from one home to another. (Chapter 6 looks at different models of family separation.)

We are asked whether it isn't unfair to expect children to pack their things into a bag and move them to the other parent's house and then take them back again, with all the disruption that this can cause. But, again, it is important to stress that your children's experience of a situation can be managed by you and the other parent to make sure that the benefits of moving between houses – the opportunity to continue having close and ongoing relationships with both parents – outweigh the irritations of having to make that physical and emotional transition.

You can make things easier for your children in many different ways, and it can be a good idea to talk with them and find out what they find to be the most difficult aspect of moving. Try to ensure that, even if most of your child's clothing remains at one parent's house, you have at least one spare set of clothes at the other home. A pair of trainers to play football in, a set of old clothes to paint in, a rainproof coat and sets of underwear and socks are all things that can mean that you are prepared for different activities and are less likely to find yourself in conflict with the other parent because your child has ended up with paint on their new jumper or got mud all over their new trainers.

Pyjamas and other nightwear, together with toothbrushes and hygiene products, can be made available in both homes so that they do not need to be transported along with everything else. Wherever possible, reduce the amount of things that need to be transferred and make sure that you have a suitable bag to carry those things that do need to move with your children. With small children, ensure that favourite bears or comfort blankets are not forgotten.

If your children are to spend one or two days at the other parent's home, consider whether certain days may be easier for your children than others. For example, if your child has football practice after school on a Wednesday, then it may be easier for them not to be carrying their football boots and kit with them on a Tuesday night; make the night for moving Thursday.

Children can enjoy the difference

It is often assumed that moving between homes, homes that often have different expectations of behaviour or cultural attitudes, will necessarily be a difficult and confusing process for children. Our experience of working with and listening to children who move between homes is that, when handled in a sensible way, not only do children not mind the move but very often welcome and enjoy it.

Very often, the move between homes allows children a little bit of space to be different and be treated differently. For instance, children tell us that far from being concerned that their dad's house is less tidy than their mum's, it can be quite nice because 'Dad doesn't mind if we just kick our shoes off when we come in from school', or 'Mum can be a bit fussy sometimes when our bedroom is a mess, but our bedsheets always smell nice and fresh.'

The rules and ways of living are predictable and secure at both homes and the children experience the best of both and enjoy the freedom that this can bring.

Nevertheless, it is important that a shared care for your child's well-being does not fall between the cracks during the

move. It is important that some central values are maintained at both homes (see Chapter 2 for more advice) and
that information about your child's welfare is transferred
along with your child.

Learning new parenting responsibilities

'I was pretty concerned when David left. Here I was with a 15-
year-old daughter who was never shy about letting me know
what she thought about me. David had always got between us
to make sure that the gloves never really came off, and now
he wasn't going to be there to do that. I think both myself and
Stephanie were worried about that.'
Ruth

It is generally the case that while we are parenting together
with a partner, we each do the things that we feel comfortable with. We each pick up the jobs and responsibilities that
we feel capable of and divide out what's left over as best we
can.

When you separate and begin parenting on your own, it
becomes necessary for you to pick up nearly all of those roles
and responsibilities, especially if your children are with you
regularly and often. After all, there is no one but you to get
things done a lot of the time.

What mums and dads are supposed to do
Many parents find that they are having to undertake tasks
and roles that they never expected they would have to do.
So, for instance, mum may have done most of the
comforting when a child was unwell, whereas dad issued the
stern lecture when there was a bad school report.

These roles very often fall along society's gendered expectations of what it is to be a good mother and what it is to be a good father. These will be different in different cultural traditions but, largely, mothers do caring and fathers do discipline.

It is often assumed that these roles are somehow inherently male or female and that we are, somehow, born with the tools to carry out these 'natural' roles. In fact, this is not the case at all. We learn these roles through our experiences of being parented, reinforced by expected cultural norms. It is not the case that men are naturally the breadwinners and that mothers are the providers of care. These are things that we learn as part of our socialisation process.

As children, our girls are given dolls to look after and prams to push them around in. Boys are given toys that reflect the world of work. Our sex – whether we are male or female – is largely fixed. Our gender – the way that we learn to behave as men or women – is not. In other words, we can choose any of the parenting roles and responsibilities that we want to.

In most industrialised countries, the division of responsibilities in family life at the beginning of the twenty-first century is very different to how it looked at the beginning of the twentieth. The influence of feminism on the family and the world of work in the last century radically transformed our expectations of what was acceptable for men and women to do both inside and outside the family. And yet, despite this cultural shift, many mothers and fathers still undertake a fairly 'traditional' parenting role. This means that your children may very well experience your parenting as coming from a particular gendered expectation.

The more that parenting roles were divided while you were parenting together, the more difficult it may be for you to adjust to parenting alone and for your children to adapt to

163

the new situation. It is, therefore, important for you to think about the things that your children need from you in terms of care and attention and to consider whether you need to learn some new parenting skills.

Parenting together, apart

At the same time, however, it is important for you to recognise that, as your children's parents, although you may be living apart, you can still provide parenting together. While children may like the idea that they can 'get away with things', the knowledge that both parents are working together to set boundaries and pass information about their children's welfare can be very reassuring.

It doesn't hurt for your child to know that a bad school report will not just stay with one parent. Neither does it harm to let the other parent know about something that has made your child feel sad or unsafe.

Think about the way you parent, consider whether there are any gaps in your skills, work out strategies to provide as much as you can for your children in terms of caring and boundary-setting and decide with the other parent where you will both need each other's help.

If your child is kicking against the boundaries you have set, you may need to 'toughen up' a little and make it clear that you are not going to be pushed into changing your position. But, if you find that you are struggling, enlist the help of the other parent rather than getting into a pointless and destructive shouting match. Similarly, if your child needs reassurance and a cuddle, it's not going to be very helpful for you to brush your child's concerns away with a cheery 'It'll be all right, don't worry.' You may need to move out of your comfort zone and actually sit and listen to your child's worries. However, if your child is still distressed, don't feel that it is a failure to contact the other parent for advice or support. In fact, by acting in this way, you are displaying to your child that you are engaging with their emotional needs and that they still have two parents who have put their child's concerns above any dislike they may have for each other.

What can I do with my children?

'I remember one Halloween, I was really strapped for cash, but the three of us made a vegetable soup and called all the things that we put in something like "eye of newt" or whatever. We made a lantern out of a turnip and some hats out of rolled-up newspaper. The kids absolutely loved it and still talk about it now even though it must be over ten years ago.'
Iain – father of two

This section is aimed largely at those parents who find themselves having to 'entertain' their children a couple of times a week or during the school holidays. But you may also find useful ideas in here even when your children live with you for most of the week.

It is a curious fact that children tend to expect their fathers to provide entertainment for them whereas they are quite content to entertain themselves while they are with their mothers. This is largely a result of the socialisation that children undergo. Mother, who in the majority of cases (gender roles can still be very traditional in a lot of households) provides most of the hands-on care for children, will very often be doing other jobs around the house and so gives the signal that a good child is one who is quiet and lets her get on with her work. Father, who may provide less hands-on parenting, will engage his children's attention by 'doing' something with them. These expectations can become

165

deeply embedded in children's psychology and their interaction with the world around them.

Many men are quite happy in this role but it can become quite tiring to keep trying to dream up new activities, especially if money is tight. There is often an increased expectation that mum will join in with activities if dad is no longer around.

One of the tricks that we have learned through our experience and through talking to other parents is that one of the simplest ways to keep your children occupied is to involve them in the work that needs doing around the house. The most obvious one is cooking.

COOKING

At various points in the day, you will need to eat and so the preparation of food can be an excellent way to keep children occupied while, at the same time, doing something practical and also teaching your children skills that will stand them in good stead for many years to come.

Children are never too young to be involved in the preparation of food. With a little help and patience, even the smallest will be able to help with weighing and stirring, washing and tasting. Find some easy recipes for biscuits or scones, buy some pizza bases and add your own toppings, make salads and lay them out on the plate in the shape of funny faces – children will almost always enjoy cooking and then eating what they have made.

We talked to one man who had what he and his children called 'theme' nights. These would involve centring the main meal on a particular country or culture. Indian food would be prepared and eaten to Indian music. A children's encyclopedia would provide some background information and, if possible, a few words of the language would be learned.

This meant that most of an afternoon and evening would revolve around the preparation and eating of a meal. It could be inexpensive and certainly cheaper than a trip into town or to the cinema.

MAKING AND GROWING THINGS

Younger children also love to make things. There is nothing nicer than an autumn walk in the park collecting leaves and seeds that can then be stuck onto paper back home. Painting and sticking will generally keep children amused for hours and, again, need not be expensive.

The time of year or particular festivals can help give you new ideas for making and painting things. There are also plenty of books in your local library that can help you find your creative side.

If you have a garden, it can be nice to give your children a small area to grow things in, especially things that they can eat. If you don't have a garden, you can grow herbs on a window sill – many shops sell pig-shaped pots and other containers designed to be attractive to children for this very purpose.

Making calendars, painting eggs, keeping diaries or scrapbooks, keeping records of the birds that visit your bird table, learning about things together, reading books to each other, making birthday cards, making up silly poems, trying simple experiments, knitting – the only thing that you need is your imagination, and your kids will love you for it!

Conclusion

Without doubt, there will be elements of your relationship with your child or children that will change for ever as a result of family separation. What, and how big, those changes are will depend not only on the circumstances you find yourself in post-separation, but how you deal with your children's needs.

You may find that you are caring for your children for most, for some, or for little of the time. If this is a change from how you have been used to discharging your parenting responsibilities, then it may come as something of a shock, not only to you, but to your children, too. If it is similar to your previous division of parenting care, then the impact may be less noticeable. However, whether you are pleased with the new arrangements or whether you feel that your wishes have been ignored, it is important that you get stuck into making sure that they work for your children. Remember, it is the quality not the quantity of parenting time that counts. If you want to change the arrangements, that's fine, but deal with it away from your children.

Your children will certainly experience a wide range of difficult emotions around the separation of their family, and it is your job to make them feel secure in their changing environment. You must remain adult and reassure your children that things will work out. Under no circumstances should you ask or allow your children to look after your emotional needs. Listen to their concerns, let them know what is happening, reassure them that they are not to blame and encourage them to talk to you about how they feel.

Whereas your new parenting role may be different from how it used to be, it doesn't automatically follow that it will be worse. Family separation can allow you to break old ways of being and think again about what you can give to your children to allow them to grow into emotionally secure and confident adults. Get some new routines in place as soon as you can and think about the ways that you are going to give your children the best that you can and how you are going to create a new, positive and fulfilling parent/child relationship.

Personal Story
Matt – dad to Luke and Jamie

My lads are aged six and eight and their mum and I separated when they were quite little. I have been on my own for most of the time since then although I have got a girlfriend now.

I was quite young when we had the boys. We had only been married for about nine months when their mum got pregnant and I don't think I reacted very well at first, I mean I was out partying every weekend while she was at home and I think that caused some longer-term problems.

When Luke was born I was pleased but not over the moon. I still felt that I was too young and both families were on to me then telling me that I had to be a responsible dad. I got a bit fed up with that bit I remember, but I did my best and gradually got used to the idea of being a dad. When Jan got pregnant for the second time, though, I went into a really deep depression. I had just started out as a club DJ and I was really into the scene. Every weekend I would be out all night on Friday working and then off somewhere else on Saturday. I just didn't want the responsibility of being a dad when I had all of that going on for me. I don't think it was very fair on Jan really but I felt justified in continuing to carry on as though I was single; I had always said that I wasn't really keen on children so I felt that if she wanted them then she would have to look after them.

The summer that Jamie was born I was in Ibiza having a

really great time. I went there every other weekend to work and loved every minute of it. As it paid well Jan didn't have any complaints, apart from being left on her own every other week, but I know she was really unhappy about it underneath.

Anyway I was in Ibiza for the weekend when Jan called and said the baby was on its way. I was really cheesed off because I had promised I would go back if she went into labour. I managed to get a flight back and arrived in time to be with her when Jamie arrived, but things weren't right for us at all by then and I think we both knew it was going to fall apart.

When Jamie was just about a year old we sat down and had a big talk. Jan said she'd had enough of me never being there and that she would rather I wasn't there at all than in and out like a lodger. I think I was relieved although I wasn't prepared for how I really felt when I actually moved out. I was stunned, absolutely stunned. I wandered around for weeks afterwards like someone lost, I wasn't interested in my old lifestyle any more, I didn't want to be off on a plane to Ibiza every other weekend and I was just horribly lonely.

I had been seeing the boys for a couple of hours on a Saturday for the first few weeks but then I realised that I missed them really badly. I couldn't work it out at first but when I realised what it was that was making me so unhappy I just rang Jan and asked her if I could see them some more. She was a bit reluctant; I think she was worried that I wouldn't know what to do with them as I had had so little experience of really looking after them.

Anyway I got my place organised for them coming to stay overnight once a week. We put some futons down on the floor of my box room; there was no space for anything else but it didn't matter, it was a good-enough bedroom for the boys and they loved it. I got them some Batman quilts and a couple of plug-in nightlights, and every time they stayed over we would play Batman and Robin before bed, jumping about all over the quilts until they were exhausted. I think those nights were the very happiest I had been since I moved out of the house and I started to feel a lot better about life.

After a few months of them staying over one night each week I asked Jan if I could have them for a couple of nights. I think she was glad of the rest as the boys were really lively at that time. Also she was getting involved with someone new and the boys being with me meant that she could have the space to do that. I was so glad that I was as involved as I was by then because I was really worried that I might be replaced by anyone Jan met. By this time, though, me and the boys were getting along a treat and I even took them over to Ibiza with me for a weekend in the sunshine, which they absolutely loved.

Now they live with me for two nights every week. We have an arrangement where I have them Friday and Saturday night one weekend and then Monday and Tuesday night after the following weekend. I talk to both of them every other night and Luke now has a mobile phone and he sends me text messages to let me know how things are going at school.

I think I owe a lot to Jan for believing in me and for wanting to share our boys with me. I wasn't a fantastic dad to start with and I was an even worse partner. It was her understanding and willingness to try out a new way that meant that I could get set up with having the boys regularly. Also, when I panicked about things, such as when Jamie wouldn't eat anything because he had toothache, I was able to ring Jan and she gave me some advice instead of telling me I was useless or getting panicky herself. I think the trust that she had in me meant that I could really get to grips with being a dad by myself and start enjoying it rather than worrying about it.

I love my lads deeply and I think that being their dad has been the best thing ever. We still play Batman and Robin before bed and their futons still fill the whole of the box room, so I have made a hanging rail for their clothes that is suspended from the ceiling. They love that and the fact that my house is somewhere that they can go a bit wild in if they want to. I'm a bit more laid-back than their mum so dinner is usually in front of the TV and things are usually a bit of a tip. But they go to bed on time and they get to school on time in clean clothes so it's not all chaos.

Chapter 5

Your Children and Their Other Parent

'My God! When I found out what he had done, I was so angry that I thought that I wouldn't care if I never heard of him again. But I felt that it was important for our daughter still to see us both, and I know that he wanted to keep being a father to her but I just didn't want to have to deal with him at all. The trouble is that once you've had a child with someone, you can never really get away from them. They're always there even if it's just a memory or a question that your child has. Because our daughter was still seeing her father every week, it was impossible for me to ignore the fact that he was still important in her life, and if she was going to get the parenting that she needed to keep her safe and emotionally secure, we were going to have to find some way of communicating.'
Shazia – separated for two years

Making the relationship between your children and the other parent work

Separating from a partner or spouse can be one of the most distressing events that we will ever experience in our lives.

Very often, it will be accompanied by a betrayal or a hurt that you may never properly recover from. The separation – the physical moving away from each other – may, itself, come with high levels of anger and bitterness. Who was the perpetrator of the wrong? Who was the victim? Who should move out of the family home? Why did you leave it until now to tell me this? All of these things may leave you feeling that you never again want to have to have dealings with this person. Add to that the fact that you have had a child or children together and the hurt can be magnified many times.

Paradoxically, this added 'complication' is the thing that means that, however hard you try, you will never really be able to free yourself from the relationship with that person. Whether you like it or not, your children will either still experience them on an ongoing basis or, even where they don't, will have a memory and an internalised relationship with them. This is something that you will have to face up to and, if you want your child or children to grow up feeling emotionally safe and rounded, will need to handle with care.

Making the transition from parenting together to being parents together but living separate lives is not an easy one. As well as adjusting to your life without your ex-partner, you will need to deal with your new parenting role and the potential changes in your relationship with your children and, no less importantly, their relationship with their other parent.

Your children have the right to a relationship with their other parent

Whatever the circumstances of your separation, regardless of how you see your life in the future, your children have the right to a relationship with their other parent.

The nature of that relationship may vary according to

circumstances but, unless there are concerns about safety (in which case it is vital that you seek help from the appropriate bodies), that relationship should be centred around the needs of your children not on yours or the other parent's.

Children are not possessions

It may seem unnecessary for us to say it, but we will anyway! Children are not possessions to be fought over and divided up. They are precious, growing, sensitive young people who require you both to put their needs before your own. Unless there are genuine concerns about their well-being or safety, it is not acceptable for you to prevent your children from seeing their other parent. Neither is it acceptable for you to make it impossible for your children to continue to have a relationship with you by walking away from their lives.

Although it may have been the case in the past, most cultures in the UK, Europe, the United States, Australia, New Zealand and South Africa do not consider children to be 'possessions'. Nevertheless, in too many of the cases that we come into contact with, it is clear that parents can find it difficult to discuss post-separation care arrangements without treating them as such. In other words, parents demand their 'rights' to see their children in the same way as they might demand their right to half of the savings.

Interestingly, we also deal with parents who act as though their children are a possession that they no longer have an interest in. So, just as they are not interested in having half of the furniture because they have no need of it in their new life, they see no place in their new lives for their children and simply walk away.

Don't rush to the barricades

The battle over 'access' to children (what we prefer to call 'parenting time') has become an extremely divisive matter in recent years to the point where it has spilled over into the legal and political arenas and made headline news in several countries. Many fathers, who have begun to take a more significant role in parenting, feel that they should not simply be sidelined when families separate. Likewise, many mothers, who have grown up in a society that still considers women to be the primary carers for children, can feel threatened by this perceived encroachment on their parenthood. Invariably, the discourse centres on the 'rights' of parents, with each demanding that they be treated 'justly'.

It is hardly surprising that people who are experiencing the attendant trauma and chaos of family separation feel like this. A world of stability and relative certainty, where your parenting role may never have been questioned, has suddenly been transformed into a world where all the things that you have taken for granted – including the role that you play in your children's lives – seem suddenly to be insecure and subject to question.

Given this internal anxiety, coupled with external pressure to conform to cultural and peer expectations, it is little wonder that parents, in spite of their best intentions, can find themselves throwing up the barricades and reaching for the megaphones, 'I demand my right to . . .'

We feel that it is important to recognise and acknowledge that family separation can, and frequently does, produce all kinds of injustices, unfairness and genuine grievances. As practitioners working with people who are experiencing the effects of family separation at the sharp end, we know only too well what damage such injustices can have on a parent's health and well-being. However, in all of this, what counts more than anything else is the need to provide a stable and secure environment in which your children can grow.

Try to move beyond injustice

We are working, not in some ivory tower, but in the real world where we encounter people's hurt on a daily basis. We consider it to be both wrong and unhelpful to pretend that people's experiences should be ignored or that individuals should simply put them to one side. In our work, we attempt to offer practical help where possible to change the circumstances that have led to an injustice, to acknowledge a parent's hurt or frustration where that is justified but, equally important as far as the parent is concerned and essential as far as their children are concerned, we try to help parents to move beyond their own experience and to focus in on their child's or children's experience.

This is not a one-off, once-and-for-all task and we don't pretend that it is easy, but each time you are able to achieve it, you empower yourself and make the daily life of your child or children that much less difficult.

Agreeing parenting time

Our whole philosophy is based on the evidence that children fare best when they have regular ongoing relationships with both parents that are flexible and responsive to the children's changing needs. It need hardly be stated, then, that for this to be possible, children must be able to share time with both of their parents.

Many people in the UK and elsewhere, particularly those working with and for groups that we might loosely call 'fathers' rights' groups, are beginning to argue that there should be a presumption in family law that 'contact' time should be split on a 50/50 basis. We, however, remain wholly unconvinced by this argument as, if we are to place the needs of children rather than those of parents at the centre of post-separation arrangements, what is important is to assess children's needs for care and then work out how best they can be met.

These arrangements will, of course, vary according to the circumstances that you find yourselves in and may well be influenced by your previous arrangements or the ability that you both feel that you have to provide ongoing care. However, at all times, you must try to detach your feelings about the other parent from the feelings that your children will have about their other parent and their continued need to experience parenting input from you both.

Deal with your feelings about the other parent

For your children to adjust to the new post-separation environment, it is vital that you allow your children to have a free and uncomplicated relationship with their other parent. This can feel like a difficult project – after all, we may be talking about the person that you like least in the world – but you are not being required to like the other parent. You need only ensure that your feelings for the other parent do not interfere with your child's or children's ongoing need to have a relationship with you both. Your starting point is learning to be able to disentangle what you feel about the other parent from what your child or children need.

The nature of your separation may well determine how easy it is for you to adapt to the relationship between your child or children and their other parent after you part. If the separation has been amicable and something that you have both wanted or recognised as having been inevitable, then it may well be that your children's relationship with the other parent presents you with no problems at all. The difficulties arise when you have grown to dislike the other parent or they have hurt you in some way.

It is vital that we learn to identify and separate out our feelings for the other parent from our children's feelings for them. Just because we are angry, hurt or humiliated does not mean that we should expect our children to feel the same. More than that, it is positively harmful for us to require them to.

Let your children love the other parent

The task at hand is to draw a very distinct line between our relationship with our ex-partner or spouse and our children's continued relationship with them as their other parent. We must allow our children to experience their other parent free from any negative feelings that we may have for them. To interfere with that relationship can be one of the worst things that we can do to our children.

Just because this task is important doesn't necessarily mean that it is an easy one to master. In fact, depending on the level of animosity between yourself and the other parent, it may be something that you will need to battle with for as long as your children are children. Stick at it, though. The rewards may not be obvious – indeed, you may wonder whether the sacrifice of keeping quiet when you really want to shout and scream about the other parent is anything other than martyrdom – but it is one of the most precious gifts that you can give to your children.

Allowing your children to love the other parent should not be seen, necessarily, as a passive process. In order for them to feel comfortable in their relationship with the other parent, you will need to allow them to talk about that person without them experiencing your hurt or anger. You must make it possible for your children to be able to talk about their life with their other parent. You must be able to deal with your own emotional processes away from your children, and you must never, ever require your children to take sides or carry the burden of your separation. Remember that you are the adult and it is your job to make your children feel safe, not the other way round.

Keep your children away from your negative feelings

If your children's other parent hurt you very badly or if you have come to realise that you actually never liked them very much in the first place, it may be difficult to keep those feelings away from your children. Despite your best intentions, you may find yourself calling them names in front of your children, criticising their lifestyle or parenting qualities or, through the tone of your voice, make it pretty obvious that you think they are an all-round waste of space!

Having those feelings does not make you a 'bad' person; they are quite normal and may help you to survive the pain that you will be experiencing. But it is important to understand the damaging effect that expressing them in front of your children will have on their long-term psychological well-being.

Younger children, especially, have an unconditional loving relationship with both of their parents; they love their parents not for any reason other than that they *are* their parents. Even where one of those parents is absent, either because they have never been present or because they have died, children will fantasise about that parent in a wholly positive way. It is, therefore, extremely confusing and distressing for children to hear their parents engaging in name-calling or other undermining behaviour. It can be the cause of serious conflictual feelings – 'I love my dad but why is he calling my mum names?' The long-term psychological effects of this are enormous and they should not be ignored however angry you may feel.

Unburden the hurt away from your children

If you have feelings of anger or hurt, you will need to express them. Not doing so will make your recovery all the more difficult and risks their expression at an inappropriate time or in a way that is harmful to your children.

Ask a friend to let you get things off your chest or consider the possibility of getting professional help, such as a counsellor, if you can access one. Failing that, think about writing all your negative feelings down. Expressing thoughts on paper can be a really powerful way of dealing with things and can stop them going round and round inside your head. Many people find that it never hurts to have a pen and paper by the side of the bed for when they turn out the lights and find themselves overwhelmed with feelings of anger and grief. Chapter 1 has lots more information and ideas to help you to deal with your feelings.

Accept the other parent's role

There are things that we provide for our children that go almost unnoticed; things such as the reassurance we provide when things go wrong or the praise when things go well. Children experience these things differently from each parent and will tend to look to one or other for a particular response. They will also derive a great deal of security from the reinforcement of a response from one parent by another.

In other words children enjoy a wide range of interactions with both parents that can be provided individually or together.

You may consider that the other parent lacks a good many parenting skills. You may be right, but that doesn't mean that they don't provide anything for your child or children and, however hard it may be, you must accept that the other parent still has a role in your children's lives.

You don't still need to like the other parent

Accepting that the other parent has a continued role to play in your children's lives is not the same as being required still to like or admire that person. Your children do not need to hear you praising the other parent or extolling their virtues. After all, if you both thought each other so wonderful, why did you split up in the first place? What your children need is for you not to undermine their other parent.

Try to separate out what you feel about the other person as an ex-spouse or partner from what you feel about them as a parent. Think about that person and the part they played in your life and the lives of your children. Think about what you wanted and expected from them as a partner and what you wanted and expected from them as a parent. Try to consider things such as those listed below and separate out which of the qualities were ones that you sought from them as a partner and those which you feel are important qualities as a parent:

• Someone who made me laugh

• Someone who was faithful

• Someone I was proud to be with

- Someone who shared my values

- Someone who treated me with respect

- Someone I enjoyed having sex with

- Someone who shared my interests

- Someone who was patient

- Someone who I could rely on

- Someone who will engage with the children

- Someone who is capable of looking after the children

- Someone who listens to the children

- Someone who will read to the children

- Someone who spends plenty of time with the children

Obviously, you will have your own list of the qualities that are important to you. However, although there is likely to be some overlap, just a brief glance at the list above shows how separate and different most parenting qualities are from those that we seek in a partner or spouse.

Now you must start to think about those parenting qualities that the other parent can still bring to your children's lives. Do they have parenting skills that you value? What do your children enjoy about their relationship with them? Are there things that they give to your children that you aren't able to?

You may find this a very difficult process to go through,

especially if that person has hurt you badly or you are in ongoing conflict with them. If you *are* finding it difficult, try this simple exercise to see if it helps.

Exercise: What do we each give to our children?

Take a piece of paper and draw a line down the middle. On one side, write down all the things that you think you do well as a parent. It may be that you sit every night with your children to read a book, it may be that you have introduced your children to wildlife, you may be really good at making sure they always have clean clothes or it could be that you rarely shout at them. Think about all the ways in which you interact well with your children and then write them down.

Next, on the other side of the sheet, write down all the things that the other parent does well. Do they make sure your children have interesting packed lunches? Do they sit up all night with the children when they are ill? Do they make the children laugh?

Me	Other parent
Give kids good food. Make sure that they are at school on time. Help them with homework.	Plays football with our son. Makes kids laugh.
	Good at stopping them from fighting.
Look after them when ill. Read with them. Take to swimming baths.	Helps them with homework. Organises the summer barbeque.

> You may find that there are a number of things that you are both equally good at. You may discover that, despite the fact that you think that the other person was a terrible spouse or partner, they actually still have some good qualities and skills that they can bring to your children's lives. At the very least, the other parent can continue to be the 'dad' or 'mum' that your children know and love.

Agree to work together

'I think what was interesting was that, once we'd decided to try and work together, things just seemed to become easier between us. I'm not saying that things were suddenly magically great or anything. I mean, I used to look at her and wonder what I'd ever seen in her! But it just seemed like the problems we'd had in our marriage became less important to us. We were less focused on them and more focused on making things right for the girls. I don't know, maybe it was because we were looking forward rather than back. I know for a fact that the girls found it easier.'

Shaun – father of two

Making the decision to work together

Hopefully, having worked through the previous exercise, you will have come to understand and accept that your child's or children's other parent still has a role to play in their lives and that this is something that is outside of how you feel about them as an ex-partner or spouse.

You will also understand that a successful and cooperative parenting relationship is possible after separation without you being required to like each other or live in each other's pockets. You should also be recognising the benefits that this will bring to your children in terms of how well they adapt to the new situation and how they will grow and develop in the years ahead. If this is where you find yourself, then you are ready to make the positive decision to work together with the other parent for the good of your children.

Think of this as a choice. Think of it as something that you have decided to do for the best of motives. Be determined. Be positive. Recognise the benefits to your children and the possibility of a happier future for everyone concerned.

Taking the first steps in working together

How you take the first steps in working together will very much depend on the current state of relations between yourself and the other parent.

If you are managing not to get into deep conflict, then progressing towards a new, post-separation parenting relationship may not feel too daunting. You may be able to discuss, immediately, the ways in which you feel you will be able to cooperate and the ways in which you are both going to contribute to the ongoing well-being of your children.

However, if your relationship is more strained or is sinking into bitterness and conflict, you will need to be more careful about how you proceed. Don't expect that, because you have decided to find a way of working together, the other parent will either be in the same place or will immediately be won round to your way of thinking. Indeed, it may well be that to reach your desired goal will take a great deal of patience and perseverance.

If you are finding it difficult to take the first few steps in working together, look for easy opportunities to achieve relatively easy successes. Perhaps you could share thoughts on your child's school report or make an agreement that your child may make a phone call to the other parent at the same time each night regardless of where the child is sleeping. Whatever you do, stick at it and be patient; if you succeed, your children will benefit from your efforts for the rest of their lives.

Make communication a priority

Good communications between you and the other parent can mean that your children need experience only a minimum amount of discomfort and awkwardness in the new separated family. If you and the other parent are on good terms after the separation, then it may be possible to have completely free and uncomplicated discussions about your children's needs and well-being. But if things are more strained between you, you may need to establish more formal methods of communicating important information.

If you feel that you can discuss things face to face, you may need to make this a more formal process than you have been used to. Try to agree a time and a place – if needs be, away from your children – where you can discuss all the important things about your children's lives.

If a phone call is easier than meeting face to face, then that's fine. Again, agree a time to do this and try to make it businesslike. Some parents even use the electronic media such as email or SMS text messaging to make sure that information gets through. The important thing is to understand the importance of good communication and agree with the other parent how you are going to bring this about.

Why it is important to exchange information

As parents living together, information about the well-being of your children is very often passed between you without you even realising that that is what is happening. General discussions together will usually mean that you both have the information that you need to ensure that your children's needs are met.

Sometimes, one parent takes a greater role in one particular aspect of their children's lives than the other and the need for you both to have detailed information about that aspect is less important.

When you are parenting separately, it becomes more difficult to pick up on the important things that are happening in your children's lives as the opportunities for casual conversations and the chances of tuning in to other conversations around the house are no longer present. In addition to that, it is likely that you will need to take an active role in parts of your children's lives that you previously left to the other parent. It is likely, therefore, that you will need to make a conscious decision to share information about your children with the other parent and, as we have discussed, if this is to work successfully and with as little stress as possible, you may well need to initiate formal mechanisms for doing so.

Your decision to exchange information with the other parent provides two important things for the continued well-being of your children. First, it ensures that key pieces of information do not fall through the gaps between you and the other parent and, second, it provides your children with a sense of continuity and a feeling that they still have two parents who care about them.

Significant information to exchange

At a time when your children will be experiencing a high degree of anxiety about the separation and, indeed, what the future holds, you both have a responsibility to make sure that you get your communications systems right. A failure to pass the necessary information between you could mean that things such as a drop in school attendance, experimentation with alcohol or drugs and many other types of dangerous behaviour may not be properly addressed and dealt with.

Significant information that needs to be passed between parents will be things such as:

Issues around health These should include any illnesses or health concerns and things such as the results of trips to the dentist. Very practical issues such as ensuring that medication is passed along with the instructions on how it should be taken must not be overlooked. It may also be important to monitor your children's health as a measure of how they are adjusting to the family separation. You may discover that your children are reporting headaches, sickness or other symptoms. These may be the result of stress caused by the separation or may be an unconscious response to the fear of being left – younger children will often feel ill, or even feign illness, in order to keep an eye on your whereabouts, something that they can't do if they are at school. You and the other parent need to look out for patterns of illness.

Reactions to the separation Younger children, in particular, may find it difficult to articulate their feelings consistently, and so it is important to pass this information between you so that you can both respond accordingly. Be careful! You must ensure that this is not conveyed in a manner that makes your children feel as if their reactions are, somehow, wrong.

Unusual behaviour If your children occasionally behave in an unusual manner while you are with them, you may decide that it is insignificant. However, it is important to establish whether this behaviour persists while they are with the other parent. In this way, it is possible to decide whether there is a pattern that may give rise to greater concern, whether the actions of one or other of you is giving rise to the change in behaviour or whether, as you first thought, the change in behaviour is unimportant.

School attendance and performance There are a number of important reasons for passing on information about school, not least because children, regardless of whether they are in a family that is living together or one that is living apart, are renowned for not remembering to pass on important news about school! As a result of work commitments and other similar factors, it is very common for one parent to have a higher level of contact with the school than the other. Many schools do not have particularly good systems in place for keeping both parents up to date with their children's progress, and so the responsibility falls on you, as parents. Don't wait to be asked. Don't wait to be told. Just pass the information on. Changes in progress at school can be one of the key indicators as to how well a child is adjusting to the new circumstances, and so it is vital that you share as much information with the other parent as possible. It is also worth pointing out that younger children, in particular, will derive a great deal of comfort from being able to share their successes with you both and understand that you are both dealing with any concerns together.

Information about other family members Don't forget that your children's family may extend beyond you and the other parent. Particularly in the early days after separation, children will find security in knowing that this wider kinship is still recognised by you both.

Decisions that your children have made for themselves
You may need to help children to pass on decisions that they have made about their lives to the other parent if they lack the confidence to do so on their own behalf; this is especially so if they feel that their decision may make the other parent unhappy or angry.

It may be something relatively simple like deciding to become a vegetarian or a desire to stop playing a musical instrument. If you are in any doubt how happy your children are about announcing such decisions, step in and help them. If you are unsure whether they will welcome your intervention, ask them.

However, it may be something more complicated like a child's desire to change or reduce the parenting time arrangements. If this is the case, then you must proceed very carefully and make sure that your help isn't seen as conspiracy by the other parent. Whatever you do, make sure that your children aren't going to be caught in crossfire.

Decisions that you have made on your children's behalf If you make a decision about your children's lives, it generally needs to be communicated to the other parent as this allows them the chance to bring consistency into your parenting. This may be around changes to bedtime or sanctions you have imposed where you have had concerns about your child's behaviour. Obviously, you should use common sense and not pass on every little detail and overload the other parent with useless information – this may just seem to be being fussy. You must also be prepared for the other parent to disagree with, and not implement, your decision while your child is with them.

Don't forget that you should try to agree all major parenting decisions with the other parent if at all possible as this gives children a sense of continuity and ongoing care. However, even here, you may need to be prepared for the other parent to want to do things differently from you.

Learning new ways of communicating

While you lived with the other parent, you probably had fairly clearly defined ways of communicating. You may have sat and discussed things every now and then, you may have passed information as you went through your everyday routines, you may even have bellowed at each other when you were so angry that you could no longer keep your peace!

Whatever method you used in the past, it is likely that if your intention to communicate well is to become a reality, you will both need to learn new communication skills.

Learn to communicate clearly

One key thing to be aware of when thinking about learning to communicate clearly is that the communication patterns that you and the other parent will have established when you lived together may well have been one of the causes of your separation. You may have felt unable to ask for what you needed while you were in the relationship or you made your partner feel that you were angry with them when you were not.

Try to think about the ways that you exchanged information and made joint decisions in the past to see if there were patterns that led to arguments or resentments. It is important that old, destructive patterns are not carried forward in your new parenting roles; if they are, it may well be that your children's lives will be blighted by conflict and a division that makes them feel lost in the space between their two parents.

What kind of a communicator are you?

Broadly speaking, there are three ways in which we conduct our communications with other people. These are:

1. **Aggressive** Typically, this manner will be demanding, unable or unwilling to recognise the other person's position, and will be, generally, confrontational.

2. **Passive** This manifests itself in an inability to articulate needs, putting the other person's wishes above your own or not feeling that you have the 'right' to ask for the things you want.

3. **Assertive** This technique involves identifying your needs and asking very clearly that they be met, not by demanding or through subterfuge but because you feel that what you want is reasonable and that it should be discussed.

What communication styles should be avoided?

If you are aggressive and the other parent is passive then, in the short term, you will 'win' and they will 'lose'. If the other parent is aggressive and you are passive, then they will 'win' and you will 'lose'. If you are both aggressive, there will be a perpetual war, and if you are both passive then there is likely to be considerable ongoing confusion.

The truth is that in each of these situations your children will lose. They will see the destructive nature of the inequality of power between their parents and they will see the unhappiness that this brings. They may resent you for the aggression that you display towards their other parent or they may resent the fact that you have not clearly communicated what they needed or wanted. Don't forget that it is for their continued well-being that you have both decided to pass information and make decisions about their lives between you.

The other major problem if one parent always comes out on top is that this very often leads to the other parent taking their revenge at a later date or in a different situation; revenge is never helpful in building post-separation parenting relationships that put children's needs first!

HOW BAD COMMUNICATION PATTERNS CAN CAUSE PROBLEMS

Let's take a simple example

Dad demands that his son spends Christmas Day at his house. Because of his aggressive tone, mum backs down and agrees. However, when she is away from that confrontational situation, she feels resentful at not being able to ask properly for what she wanted and for not having the opportunity or confidence to be able to articulate her son's wishes. In revenge, she makes sure that the boy doesn't have the wherewithal to buy his dad a present.

As a result of the imbalance of power and the inability of both to communicate in a constructive manner, mum is unhappy because she did not get a chance to share the day with her son, dad is angry because mum has made the boy feel awkward about not being able to give him a present, and the boy – who would have liked to have spent time with both of his parents and given each of them a present – is unhappy and angry because he did not have the chance to see one of his parents on the day and was unable to give the other parent a present. In fact, the whole day has been ruined for him because he was aware of the hostility between his parents and the shadow that it cast over what should have been a happy occasion.

Which communication techniques work best?

Have you ever smiled when you were angry? Have you ever displayed anger when, actually, you were very frightened? Do you ever laugh and make jokes when inside you are crying? Have you ever accused another person when, in reality, you feel guilty? These are known as 'masking techniques', in other words, we are hiding our true emotions – often to protect ourselves – by displaying the opposite. If you are going to be able to communicate in a free and constructive manner, then you are going to have to learn to avoid the signs of masking and find ways to be more honest about your feelings. After all, if the person that you are communicating with is to understand truly what you are feeling and saying, you have to make it clear. It's no good expecting them to be able to read your mind, no matter how well they know you.

Earlier, we identified aggressive, passive and assertive as the three main ways that we communicate with others. We have looked at how aggressive and passive methods usually lead to difficulties for you, the other parent and your children. It is important, then, that you learn to use the third technique when discussing and making decisions about your children's lives – assertive.

Some people confuse assertiveness with aggression – don't! Aggression is about demanding and imposing, assertiveness is about the clear and straightforward statement of your feelings and wishes.

HOW GOOD COMMUNICATION TECHNIQUES CAN REDUCE PROBLEMS

We saw previously how passive and aggressive methods of communication lead to conflict and unhappiness for both the parents and the child. Let's look, now, at how it might have been different if one or both of the adults had been able to communicate in an assertive manner.

Dad would like to spend some time with his son on Christmas Day; mum would too and the boy would like to spend time with them both. Dad states his wishes clearly but not aggressively. Mum, not feeling threatened and having learned to be assertive, is able to say what she would like to happen and is able to relay her son's wishes. It is clear that for everyone to get something they want there will need to be compromise. After some discussion, mum and dad put it to their son that he spends Christmas Eve at his dad's house and goes to his mum's house on Christmas Day, ensuring that he is there in time for Christmas dinner. Everyone is as happy with this outcome as the situation permits, and mum is more than happy to give her son a few pounds so that he can buy his dad a small present.

Exercise: Learn to be assertive

This exercise is designed to help you think about the ways in which you deal with particular situations and the techniques you can use to help you feel more in control of them. It's an exercise that you can do on your own or, if you fancy it, with a friend. These communication skills are useful in many other walks of life, not only in dealing with another parent.

While we tend to have one dominant manner in which we communicate, we may well use different styles in different situations. So, although you may be a generally passive or generally aggressive communicator in your relationship with the other parent, you may well be assertive in your work life. Begin the exercise by thinking about the ways you handle different situations. How do you communicate with the other parent? How do you speak to your children? Do you speak differently to them depending on the mood you find yourself in? Imagine that you are taking something back to a shop; do you feel comfortable asking for an exchange or for your money back? Think about being in a café or a restaurant where you are unhappy with the way you have been treated; how do you react? Do you say nothing? Are you apologetic about saying something? Do you shout and demand that something is done or do you ask, quietly but firmly, to talk to the manager?

Think about as many different potentially confrontational situations as you can and then think about the ones where you feel least in control, the ones where you feel the most uncomfortable and the ones where you struggle to say what you want to say.

It's an interesting, although little known fact that when you speak to someone face to face, the thing that they focus on least is what you say. More significant is the tone of voice you adopt and the body language you display. The pie chart over-leaf shows how important each of these factors is in making yourself understood.

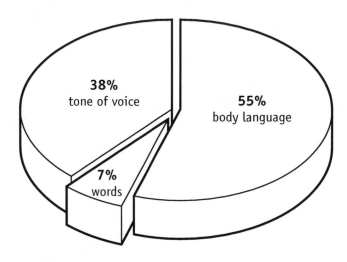

BODY LANGUAGE

With this in mind, let's start by focusing on your body language. If you are working through this exercise with a friend, position yourselves standing face to face at a comfortable distance apart. If you are doing this exercise alone, then it can help to have a large mirror in front of you so that you can see and understand your own body language. If you haven't got a mirror, face a wall to help you to imagine yourself in relation to another person. Now, practise the following to take control of your body:

Balance Put your feet flat and evenly on the floor, hip-width apart. Crossed legs give off passive signals and having your legs too far apart displays aggression.

Breathing Breathe slowly and deeply from the diaphragm. If your breathing is too shallow, it will be difficult to control your voice. This can lead to a weak and passive sound or you may overcompensate and your voice will have an aggressive edge.

Posture Adopt an 'open' body posture. Keep your arms by your sides rather than across your chest (which can appear defensive or hostile) and keep your head up. Keep your hands open – a clenched fist gives aggressive signals. Take care to make sure you are comfortable, though, you are not trying to stay rigid!

Eye contact Look the other person in the eye while being careful that you are not staring. If you feel uncomfortable with this, it can help to focus on the bridge of the nose, between the eyes.

Personal space Think about the distance between yourself and the other person. If you are too close, especially if you are bigger, they may feel threatened. If you are too far away, you may appear to be timid.

How did adopting this body language feel? How did it look? Think about your reflection or ask the person you are doing the exercise with. How did it make them feel? Were they aware of any changes in their body language as a result of the way you were standing? If you felt foolish or uncomfortable, don't worry, with a little practice you will start to feel less awkward and more in control of your body.

TONE OF VOICE

Now practise your tone of voice. Choose a scenario that you are going to practise with. Try using a situation that you identified as being one where you feel less comfortable (if you are working with a friend, perhaps they could take on the role of the other parent).

Decide on a phrase that you are going to use. Here, we are not so concerned with *what* you say so much as *how* you say it. If you can't think of what to say, you can use something as simple as 'No' or 'Please don't do that' or even 'Please will you pass the biscuits.'

Your tone should be clear, firm and controlled but *not* aggressive. This may take a while to get the hang of, but keep trying. Don't forget, also, what you have learned about body language.

WORDS TO USE

Having learned about and practised some body language and voice techniques, you can now focus on the right kind of words to use to convey what you want in a clear, non-aggressive or passive manner. Here are some things to bear in mind:

Speak personally Use 'I' not 'you'. For example 'I would rather you didn't do that' instead of 'You always do that.'

Be direct Say exactly what you mean and try not to anticipate the response that you are going to get. Being direct requires the other person to deal with what you have said rather than allowing them space to evade it.

Be specific Don't make generalisations. If the other parent has been late to a hand-over on three occasions say 'This is the third time that you have been late' rather than 'You never get here on time.'

Say what you feel If you are frightened, say so. If you welcome the way the other person is responding to you, tell them.

Ask questions Say what you need to say and then ask the other person how they feel about what you have said. Be prepared to acknowledge their point of view, and where it is reasonable and appropriate, alter your position.

Extra tip Although you cannot be seen, adopt the body language techniques while you are on the telephone – it will help you to say what you want in an assertive manner.

A brief note on how men and women communicate differently

Particular problems can arise between men and women because they very often tend towards different ways of communicating. That is not to say that men and women are necessarily born with different communication techniques; it comes about through the ways we are brought up, our socialisation and the different environments we inhabit as adults. Neither does it mean that all men and all women communicate in an exclusively male or female way at all times.

However, men may wish to note that because women generally tend towards a long narrative – 'I'm having my hair done at ten o'clock, it was the only time they could fit me in, and I know that you like to have a lie-in on Saturdays, but it would be helpful if you could pick Helen up at nine, or would that mean you won't be able to go out on Friday night ...?' – does not necessarily mean that they are trying to run your life for you or pester you. And women may find it useful to understand that men's tendency towards brevity – 'Can you have Helen at ten this Saturday?' – does not necessarily mean that they are disinterested or bored.

Don't ask your children to communicate on your behalf

It can be tempting to let or ask your children to do the communication on your behalf. This should be avoided as much as possible. The very practical reason for this is that children aren't the best at remembering to pass information on or the best at getting the message right, even if they do! But, more significantly, in requiring your children to become the means by which information is passed, you are asking your children to share the responsibilities of parenthood.

The reason that you are sharing information about your children is to make sure that they remain safe and have all of their needs met. It gives children a sense that they are being cared for and about; that over their heads, dad and mum are looking after them. Asking them to be part of that process gives the message that you are not sufficiently adult to put your children's needs ahead of yours and that you are asking them to make that OK for you. It rarely is.

Never require your children to keep secrets from the other parent. This can cause huge problems of loyalty for your children and it just isn't fair to put them in that position. Neither is it a good idea to ask your children to spy on your behalf. If you want to know something about the other parent, ask them yourself. Again, children may experience your interrogation of them as a requirement to be disloyal to their mum or dad.

Supporting each other to parent

Research shows that the less conflict there is between parents after separation, the more likely it is that your children will adapt to the new situation and continue to thrive. Clearly, the deliberate or unintentional undermining of the other parent will work against this, but as well as ensuring that you aren't harming your children's relationship with the other parent, if you are both able to, you can actively support each other in your parenting. This may be done in as many different ways as you think are possible and appropriate; the only thing that you need to be cautious of is not giving conflicting messages to your children – if you have separated, don't give them confusing messages that may lead them to wonder if you are getting back together when you are not.

The more you are both able to support each other's parenting role, the more you are helping your children to deal with the separation. And the more you help your children to deal with the separation, the happier and more secure your children will feel. In other words, you don't need to feel that you are supporting the other parent for their benefit in order to understand that doing so is in the best interests of your children.

Very simple acts of cooperation can help your children get the best from their relationship with their other parent. Making sure that you are communicating important messages, discussing your children's particular concerns or desires and ensuring your children's material comfort in their relationship with the other parent (making sure they have the clothes that they need and the toys they like) are all things that it's possible to achieve if you are both willing to make the effort.

Make it as easy as you can for your child

'I don't see why I should help him make things all right; he was the one who left. It serves him right if she kicks off because she hasn't got her straighteners there. I bought them!'

Many of the parents that we work with find it very difficult to disentangle what they feel for the other parent with what their children feel for them. This can make it that much harder for them to facilitate the transition from one home to another without resentment.

Certainly, this can mean that the other parent isn't able to provide as comfortable an environment or experience for your children as you do. You may feel a sense of satisfaction about this or feel that it will somehow make your children appreciate you more than they do the other parent. In fact, what you are doing is making your children's lives miserable in order that you can exact a little bit of revenge on the other parent. Your children will not thank you for it.

Don't let pride or anger or resentment get in the way of ensuring that your children have as happy, safe and secure lives as possible whether they are with you or the other parent.

Facilitate communication between your children and the other parent

Making communication between your children and the other parent as straightforward and easy as possible should be a fairly easy thing to achieve. However, it is important that you pay attention to the details if this is going to work as smoothly as your children need it to. Particularly with young children, don't leave them to be solely responsible for organising communication with the other parent. This means making sure that they are in a position to contact the other parent, have the means to do it and, if necessary, are reminded to do it.

In practice, you should agree when (what time of the day, what days in the week, and so on) and how (telephone, email, SMS text, and so on) your children will communicate with their other parent and make sure that this is honoured. If, because you are out for the day or your child is watching something special on television, the communication is not possible at the allotted time, make sure that the other parent knows – if possible, in advance. You may not particularly wish to speak to the other parent to change the arrangements, but failure to do so may mean that your child has to deal with the displeasure of the other parent.

It is also your responsibility to prompt your children to write birthday and other greeting cards, whenever it is traditional to do so. You may not care that not doing so may upset the other parent, but it may well upset your child, too.

It can be tempting to try to listen in on telephone calls or look at emails; don't! Unless you have some extremely serious concerns, it is important that you give your children the space to be able to have a private and personal relationship with their other parent. If you do overhear a conversation, by accident, don't be looking for reassurance about your own parenting. It can hurt a little when you have spent the day with your children at the seaside, followed by a meal out and an evening at the cinema and it is never mentioned in the phone call to the other parent. Your children may choose not to tell the other parent about it, either because they prefer to keep their two worlds separate or because they don't want to feel like they are asking their parents to compete with each other. Don't forget, children can be very sophisticated in their understanding of adult relationships and are also very loyal and reluctant to hurt either of you.

What to do if it all goes wrong

Sometimes, the split between yourself and the other partner is so acrimonious that it seems almost impossible to facilitate your child's relationship with the other parent. We meet parents who are so hurt and angry that they can't bear to have anything to do with each other. In cases such as these, we try to do intensive work with each parent to help them move beyond this. However, we recognise that this can take time and, indeed, may never be fully resolved.

The Parenting Phone Call

In many of the most conflictual situations, we recommend what we call the Parenting Phone Call or Scripted Phone Call. This is where we instigate a prescriptive phone conversation that is businesslike and passes the vital information between the two parents. If a telephone call is likely to be stressful and will inflame the situation, parents are advised to use email, if it is available to them.

There are strict rules about the content of the calls. These are:

1. There should be no social niceties – for example, asking whether the other parent is well.

2. The discussion only deals with information relevant to the children – if one parent wishes to discuss something else, they must request another phone call.

3. The conversation will stick to a 'boundaried', pre-agreed agenda – this makes it less likely that parents will stray into more difficult territory.

4. There should be no comment about the information given – questions may be asked if clarification or further information is required.

We have found that parents can find this approach to be very helpful in moving an exceptionally difficult situation forward, and it frequently leads to better all-round communication between them.

If you are going to draw up your own Parenting Phone Call, you may wish to use a mediator to help you agree the parameters and to set the ball rolling. Your Parenting Phone Call agenda should look something like this:

- **The good stuff** This sets a positive tone at the beginning of the call. Take it in turns to pass on any information about things that should be celebrated or marked in some way; things such as good school work, passing a cycling test or baking a cake. Pass all the information that you would want to receive but be careful not to turn it into a contest.

- **Medical information** It is important that both parents are equally aware of your children's medical situations. Pass on information about illnesses, medical appointments and potential concerns.

- **School news** Tell the other parent about school performance, behaviour, concerts and such like. As mentioned previously in this chapter, schools don't always manage to give relevant information to both parents.

- **Activities** Make sure that the other parent is aware of any activities that your children may be involved in, such as trips or clubs that they have joined. Ensure that any changes to your usual routines that may arise because of your children's activities are notified and dealt with as soon as possible.

- **Care issues** It is important that issues such as bedtimes, diet and toilet training are passed between parents. This is particularly important with children under the age of five where changes to routines – for example, whether your child has an afternoon nap – occur fairly quickly and children are less able to articulate their needs for themselves.

- **Boundaries** Whereas it is unlikely that you and the other parent will have uniformity in the boundaries that you set for your children, it helps if the gap between where each of you draw your boundaries is as narrow as possible. Consistent and commonly held values help children to feel a greater sense of stability.

- **Special events** Try to agree, in advance, how you are going to manage events like birthdays. If you wish to make changes, make your request as early as possible.

- **New business** This is a chance for each of you to raise issues that have not been covered elsewhere or to give advance notice of something that you may want to deal with at a future date.

- **Next call** Agree the date and time of the next phone call and also set some rules about when it would be allowable to call in advance of this. It helps to keep you both on a businesslike footing if you phone at the same time on the same day each week or at some other regular interval; but you must agree to notify each other of things such as illness or trouble at school or with the police as and when they occur.

- **CAUTION** The Parenting Phone Call should be used only where other forms of communication are failing or where you wish to use it as a prelude to less formal information exchanges. It should be as businesslike and 'boundaried' as you can make it. You must never let the phone call descend into arguments or debates about the reasons behind your separation or even into discussions about how you are feeling. The Parenting Phone Call is about your children, not you. If you find yourself getting bogged down, ask the other parent to agree to discuss the problem at a later date or even later the same day. Try to agree a signal that terminates the phone call so that it does not drag on. If the phone call starts to get out of hand, tell the other parent that you are not comfortable with the way things are going. If there is no change, warn the other parent that you are going to end the call. Then, and only then, you should hang up.

Minimum Standards Compact

If all else fails, then it can be a good idea to agree what we have called a Minimum Standards Compact. This is a simple agreement between the two of you that sets out the basic rules of behaviour that you will both abide by in order that your children will, at the very least, be protected from the most damaging aspects of conflictual parenting and that allows your children to continue to have a relationship with both of their parents.

This compact should be written down and signed by you both with a statement that you both agree to abide by its contents. What you agree is a matter for you, and you may wish to enlist the help of a trained facilitator to help you reach a deal. However, we would recommend that it contains, at a very minimum, the following rules and undertakings. (You may wish to use the following wording or agree your own.)

We agree, on behalf of [insert the name of your child or children], to abide by the following rules and undertakings:

1. Not to allow our feelings about each other to prevent us from providing for the well-being of [insert name(s)].

2. To allow [insert name(s)] to have a relationship with both of us.

3. To allow [insert name(s)] to love us both.

4. Not to criticise each other in front of [insert name(s)].

5. To pass all important information about [insert name(s)] between us.

Signed by [insert your names and retain a copy each].

Conclusion

Being able to put all of your own personal feelings to one side in order to allow your children to have a relationship with the other parent is not always an easy thing to do. It can become an even more difficult task when you are required to facilitate that relationship actively.

You may well have feelings towards the other parent that border on hatred and yet, if your children are going to grow up with a strong sense of security and have the support in place to enjoy their childhood and become confident competent adults, you will have to find a way to negotiate and make that relationship possible.

It is quite possible that there will be all kinds of external influences that make this more difficult – family law, interfering relatives and friends, the appearance of another partner either in your life or the life of the other parent – but you must stick to your decision to allow your children to have a relationship with the other parent and do whatever you can to make sure that this is not undermined.

It is a curious fact that you may find that you can become better parents apart than you ever were together. A significant number of the parents that we see at the Centre for Separated Families tell us that, having learned new ways of cooperating around the parenting of their children, not only do they find that they have developed a successful new businesslike relationship with the other parent, but they actually find that they are experiencing and enjoying parenting in ways that they never did when they were parenting together in the former relationship.

With determination and patience, it is possible for your children to enjoy the very best of what each of you is able to contribute so that they not only survive family separation but positively flourish in the new, child-centred relationship that you have developed between yourselves. The message is, that however disastrous your family separation may feel, it is not the separation that will harm your children but the way that both parents deal with it. You have the power to act in a way that will be positive for your children and you must resolve to do so regardless of how the other parent behaves. In doing so, you also have the power to influence the way that the other parent behaves. Your children will benefit from this for the rest of their lives.

Personal Story
Julie, mother to Samantha

I think that the worst thing was a sense of betrayal and a feeling that all of the things that we had shared together, including the birth of Samantha, were somehow tainted and could never feel the same again.

Geoff and I met through work; I worked as a supervisor in the tourism department of a local authority and he was working for a company that sold advertising space in magazines and other publications. We used to talk regularly on the phone and always had a bit of a joke and a flirt, and when we actually met for the first time, I think that we both knew that we were attracted to each other.

I don't really think that I thought anything other than it might be nice to get to know him better. I certainly wasn't looking to get married or have children at that point and, to be honest, I don't think that he was, either. I suppose it's funny how things turn out.

I'm not sure why or at what point we decided to get together properly, but I'd been sharing a flat with a couple of friends that I'd been to college with, and Geoff was still living at his parents' house; so I think that it just seemed like a natural thing to do, to try and find a flat together.

I'd never lived with a man before, although Geoff had had a brief relationship with a girl when he was 19 – I think they only lived together for a few months. I actually loved it, the whole thing of buying bits for the flat together and decorating it. I remember the fun we had trying to put up these new curtain rods that we'd bought. Geoff was hopeless; he kept drilling the holes too big and then trying to make it work by stuffing them up with matchsticks.

After we'd been together for about a year, I think that we both knew that it was something that we wanted to last. I don't think I'd ever seen myself as the marrying kind – not that I thought I'd never get married, exactly, just that it seemed like such a grown-up thing to do and I suppose that I still felt quite young and carefree.

After that, having a baby seemed like the natural thing to do. It took us quite a long time to conceive and we did wonder, at one point, whether we should see someone about it. But when I did finally get pregnant, it just felt like the most magical thing in the world. I imagine every couple feels the same, but it was if the whole of every-thing revolved around this new life that was growing inside me.

We stopped going out drinking and started eating proper meals. Geoff was so sweet, he made sure that I never did any lifting or anything like that. It got to the point where I had to tell him that I wasn't made of china!

I remember that, towards the end of my term, we took a week off and went to stay in Cornwall. It was January and we rented a flat for next to nothing. Things were very close between us and I don't think that I've ever felt closer to anybody in my life. I have this picture, in my head, of myself sitting looking out of the window watching the sea crashing up against the rocks. It was early morning and Geoff was asleep in the other room and it just felt as though everything was perfect.

Those are the things that make it so difficult; those moments that you share with someone. And it all gets wrapped up with the feelings that you have about your baby. It's difficult to explain, but those days away, that place, looking forward to the birth, being scared that we wouldn't know what to do, reading the book we had to follow the progress of the baby; all that specialness is part of Samantha, it's part of who she is.

I don't think that he's ever been entirely honest about how long he'd been seeing her but I don't think it was ever anything more than a 'fling'. I don't even know who she was. My friend saw them out together and told me and, when I confronted him about it, he only half bothered to deny it. He said that our life together had become stale and that I was more interested in Sammy than I was in him. It just sounded like an excuse at the time but maybe there was something in it; I don't know.

The thing is, I don't care how boring things were or how much he said he still loved me, what he did was wrong, very wrong. It was wrong for him to do it to me but it was even more wrong for him to do it to Sammy. She was only three and a half years old and her father was letting her down like this.

I think, at first, I wasn't angry so much as sickened. I couldn't believe that he could be so selfish or so careless with everything that we had shared together. Sammy was so young and so trusting, it still makes me feel sick when I think about it today and it's nearly three years ago.

I did think about trying to stick it out but I was so hurt by what he'd done that I could barely stand to look at him, much less live with him. In the end, I told him that I wanted him out of the house and, after a week or two at his mum's, he got himself a flat and moved himself out properly.

I think that that's when the anger really kicked in. I felt so let down and he seemed to have got off scot-free. I used to lay awake at night and wonder what he was doing and who he was with. It tormented me to think that, after all we'd been through together, he'd be sharing his bed with someone else while Sammy and I were alone in this house. He seemed to have gone off and started a new life and we were left to pick up the pieces of our old life.

In terms of him paying child support, there was never a problem. But it made me so angry that all he had to do was pay up every month and that was that. In the end, I told him that he couldn't see Sammy, which was daft when I look back on it. I was angry with him for not having put her first, but the way I expressed that was to stop him seeing her at all!

It didn't help that our parents got involved. I had my mum telling me that I should never have had anything to do with him in the first place and his mum making sarcastic comments suggesting that if I'd have looked after Geoff better he wouldn't have felt the need to stray. It was all pretty childish, looking back on it.

If I'm honest, I think it was Geoff who made the first moves to sort things out. I just couldn't get past the fact that he'd hurt me and Sammy. I felt as though he'd forfeited his right to continue being a father and I just didn't want him to have any part of her life.

He went to the Centre for Separated Families and they told him to write to me saying what he felt and what he wanted. Actually, I was pretty annoyed that he was talking to outsiders about our private business but there was something about the letter that cut through all of the hurt that I felt. I can't remember the exact phrase now, but it was something along the lines of 'Although you and I may not love each other any more, Sam still sees us as her mum and dad and I still want to be there for her.' Of course, I'd known that all along, at one level, but seeing it written down like that made me have to confront it.

I talked to a few people who'd been through similar experiences. Some said that I should just try and get whatever I could out of him, but others were more positive. Interestingly, it was someone I knew through my keep-fit club who really made me change my mind. Her husband had been killed in an accident at work and she was saying how awful it was that her son would never know his dad. I think that it made me see things from Sammy's point of view. It wasn't about what Geoff wanted or what I wanted, it was about what Sammy wanted.

Don't get me wrong, that makes it all sound very easy! It actually took a lot of hard work on both our parts to get us to where we are today.

We started by agreeing one day a week when Geoff would have Sammy to stay over – we hardly even looked at each other when it came to handing-over time. But it was daft because the poor girl was stuck right in the middle of us. She loves us both and I think it must have been awful for her not to be able to show that. She always looked so lost and little, like she wanted to please us both but had no idea how to do it. It was selfish of us, really, because we were expecting this little girl to deal with something that was nothing to do with her.

We both knew it and in the end we agreed to try to make things easier for her. Now, she stays with Geoff two nights a week. We talk to each other about Sammy when she is moving between us and we have agreed to allow and encourage her to talk about each of us when we are alone with her. You can see how much it means to her. She's so much happier and she doesn't look terrified every time Geoff and I are together. I'm glad we've made the effort. I can never forgive Geoff for what he did but Sammy doesn't need to be a part of that.

Chapter 6

Your New Separated Family

THE PHRASE 'WE will always be your mum and dad' is one that must have been repeated over and over as the divorce rates, at least in the developed world, have rocketed year on year. Since the early 1970s, when the divorce rate really began to rise, there has been a steady increase every year in the numbers of people who have filed for divorce.

For example, in 1920 in England and Wales, less than one in every thousand couples divorced. This rose to just under six in every thousand married couples by 1960. In the US the rates were higher, with just under eight in every thousand married couples divorcing in the 1920s, rising to 18 in every thousand by 1960. From 1960 onwards, however, there were marked changes in the divorce rates, which doubled in the US between 1960 and 1990 and in England and Wales where a similar trend was seen. The divorce rates for England and Wales show some similarity with those of Australia, Canada and New Zealand over the period 1960 to 1990, with a levelling out occurring in the early 1980s.

As divorce and family separation grew more common the

attitudes to it became more relaxed and children living in separated family situations were less stigmatised.

But what does it mean to children, to hear the words 'we will always be your mum and dad' and then find that the familiar ways in which you used to be mum and dad have changed for ever?

Children now have to cope with living with one parent and seeing the other occasionally, or they may find themselves living in two different homes, with two very different lifestyles. Despite your reassurances, despite the fact that many of their friends will also be living in similar situations, each child affected by family separation will have their own unique reaction to it and will adapt or not in ways that are entirely individual.

It is, therefore, your responsibility, as the parents in your children's lives, to provide the consistency, reliability and predictability that your children need in order to adapt to their new situation. Reassurance in terms of telling children that they are loved always by both of you is important, but actions always speak louder than words and if your actions show that you are ambivalent about arrangements or that you are unreliable in terms of timekeeping, children will soon begin to doubt the reality of that statement 'we will always be your mum and dad'.

There is a wealth of research across the Western world about the impact of divorce and separation on children. Statistics are often quoted about the risk to children of growing up delinquent, underachieving and leading chaotic lives. While assumptions are made about the likelihood of children living in separated family situations going on to experience difficulties in relationships in their adult lives, a closer examination of the research shows that it is not necessarily divorce and separation that have a negative impact on children but the ways in which the adults around them deal with it.

If parents cannot control the conflict and do not provide continued close relationships with children, then children appear to suffer in terms of their future potential. Most studies show that conflict between separating parents has a long-lasting effect on children if it is prolonged and children are regularly witnesses to it. Studies also show that it is the loss of contact between children and one of their parents – still overwhelmingly the father – that also has a long-lasting negative impact.

In our work with separated parents – and, indeed, as separated parents ourselves – we have always believed that children can cope with family separation without it affecting their future, if their needs are taken seriously and they feel that they are their parents' first priority. But those children who are caught in the crossfire of their parents' frustration, anger and grief and those children whose parents are not able to put them first are very definitely at risk of future problems related to family separation.

You are likely now to have arrived at a place where the dust is starting to settle and your new way of life is becoming more familiar. You may have started to use some of the advice in this book that has hopefully helped you to carve out new routines and ways of being with your children. You will be aware now of the important issues involved in building a cooperative relationship with your children's other parent and perhaps you have been able to identify what the difficulties for you personally are.

In this last chapter we are going to talk about your life as a separated family which may seem odd given that you have just gone through a process of moving out or away from your ex-partner on a physical, emotional and mental level. The term 'separated family', however, is important if you are going to be able to convince your children that you will indeed always be 'their mum and dad'.

Roles in the family

The common terms for parents who have separated are either 'lone parent', used to describe the parent with whom the children live for most of the time, or 'non-resident parent', which is used to describe the other parent. In the UK, as in the US and other Western countries, most lone parents are mothers and most non-resident parents are fathers. As separated parents ourselves we have each experienced the assumptions that people make about the labels 'lone parent' and 'non-resident parent'.

Labels can be dangerous things, because they reinforce assumptions and stereotypes, and because they force people into roles that do not reflect the reality of their situation. When we are parenting together as a two-parent family, we are beyond the scrutiny of the outside world and left very much to ourselves to decide which roles we will play in our children's lives. Sometimes we are the carer and sometimes we are the provider. Most of the time we move in and out of these roles on a daily basis, ensuring that our children get what they need in terms of food, warmth, security and love and sharing the tasks that used to be very sharply divided into gender roles.

It is rare these days for a family to have a mother who stays at home and looks after children and a father who works in the outside world and provides the discipline when he gets home. Since the 1970s we have moved a long way in terms of our expectations of ourselves as men and women to the point that many more dads are involved in the everyday details of caring for children and many more mums are out there in the world of work on a daily basis.

When we live as a two-parent family, we are free to explore these challenges and to combine our care for our children with our work outside of the home. When we separate, however, it becomes immediately apparent that even if our own attitudes to gender roles have changed, the policies and practices that affect us and the attitudes and assumptions about us have certainly not.

Being mum and dad after family separation

One of the big shocks for parents after family separation is that they are no longer the arbiters of their own lives. This is particularly the case if the family is dependent upon a low income and needs to claim tax credits or other welfare benefits. Even if there is relative wealth within the family, however, it is likely that one or both parents will experience a sudden and severe loss of control over their daily lives, their living arrangements and, particularly, relationships with their children.

Bob Geldof, whose highly publicised separation from the late Paula Yates, and who has gone on to champion the needs of fathers after family separation, describes the utter desolation that many parents feel when they find themselves living outside of the family:

> Everything can be tolerable until the children are taken from you. I cannot begin to describe the pain (of being handed) a note, sanctioned by your (still) wife, with whom you made these little things, with whom you had been present at the birth and previously had felt grow and kick and tumble and turn and watched the scans and felt intense manly pride and

profound love for before they were born, had changed them, taught them to talk, read and add, wrestled and played with, walked them to school, picked them up, made tea with, bathed and dressed and put them to bed ... a note that will allow you ACCESS to these little things that are the very best of you.[*]

This loss of control can exacerbate the conflict that has already led to the ending of the relationship between you and can mean that the opportunity to build a cooperative parenting relationship may be lost for ever. It is, therefore, something that must be guarded against between the two of you, which is not easy when emotions are running high.

In our experience, when families separate, there is an expectation of parents to retreat to sharply divided gender roles of carer and provider; this is underpinned by the divisive approach to supporting the separated family that is widespread in the UK and other countries.

But before we go on, we need to unpick some of the issues that arise from the gendered approaches to supporting separated families in the UK and other countries. These are the issues that provoked that heart-rending passage from Bob Geldof and the demonstrations from fathers for their right to have a relationship with their children after family separation.

As we have already said, there is an expectation after family separation that one parent will be the main carer while the other parent will become the main provider. There is no longer the option for parents to mix and match these roles because of the ways in which legislation underlines these expectations.

---

[*] Bob Geldof, 'The real love that dare not speak its name', in Andrew Bainham, Bridget Lindley, and Martin Richards (eds), *Children and Their Families: Contact, Rights and Welfare*, Hart Publishing, 2003.

THE EFFECTS OF CURRENT LEGISLATION

Without going into too much detail it is useful to describe the ways in which the roles of carer and provider are reinforced by legislation affecting the separated family (for example, the Child Support Act 1991). The roots of this lie within the financial support of the separated family that is framed around one parent to the complete exclusion of the other.

After family separation, one parent becomes what is called the 'parent with care'. This parent receives child benefit, tax credits if working outside of the home, income support (if applicable) and child support, which is paid to this parent by the other.

The other parent is labelled the 'non-resident parent'. As such, they receive no financial support but are assessed for the ability to pay child support to the other parent.

Now, we are not saying that all parents with care are mothers and all non-resident parents are fathers, but this is certainly the most common division in the UK, Australia and the US. In the UK, for example, only one in every ten parents with care is a father whereas in the US the figure is only slightly higher.

What we are saying is that we consider the divisive nature of the legislation surrounding separated parents and the support that is offered to them to be one of the key issues that gives rise to the problems that parents have in building cooperative relationships. And that, whereas we cannot change the law (at least not right at this moment), we can ensure that parents are made aware of the ways in which this division can undermine efforts to build an egalitarian partnership that is framed around the needs of their children.

We are not advocates of parental rights, by the way, but we are advocates of supporting parental responsibilities where possible. We think that, in the twenty-first century, it is a travesty that mothers and fathers should be forced back into outdated gender roles just because the family has separated. We believe that it is possible for mothers and fathers to share caring and providing for their children after family separation, not just when the family lives under the same roof, and we passionately believe that this should be supported financially, practically and emotionally by governments, by agencies and by society.

We believe it because we know that it is only when parents are able to move beyond these institutionalised barriers that they are able to recognise the damage that such divisions do to children who, after all, don't really care who cares and who provides; they just want to be with their mum and dad as much as possible.

But given that the current legislation remains in place, here are our top ten tips for getting beyond the barriers to co-operative parenting. If you are the parent with care, this next bit may take some swallowing because it requires you to let go of some of the control. If you are the non-resident parent, it might come as a huge relief to see your needs for support written down. Our best advice is to realise that most of these barriers are not the responsibility of your children's other parent. They are the product of outdated legislation and the continued institutionalised gender assumptions present in our society.

Hopefully, the Gender Equality Duty with effect in the UK from April 2007 might shift some of the most outdated ideas about mothering and fathering after family separation that are embedded within public policy and practice. But until this happens, you can use these ideas to help you get over the barriers to cooperation – some of which are outside of your control in terms of the law, but within your control in terms of how you deal with them together. The rest are to do with the assumptions that you may make about yourself and the ideas and opinions of other people. In our experience, everyone has something to say about parenting after separation.

Getting over the barriers to cooperation

Here are the top ten issues that get in the way of cooperation, as well as ways of dealing with them.

1. **Time with children** If you are the parent with care, recognise that you may be in a more privileged position than your children's other parent, particularly if you are living in the family home.

2. **Division of labour** If you are the non-resident parent, acknowledge that your children's other parent may be doing a lot of the humdrum work of caring for children and may well be finding it exhausting.

3. **Finances** If you are going to share caring for your children, recognise that doing so may require some adjustments in your finances in order that children benefit equally in both homes. This is something that you might have to work out together because of the ways in which the Child Support Act (1991) works. Other financial support such as child benefit cannot be split between parents, either, even if you are sharing care equally. This means that one of you is likely to receive most of the financial support while the other has to do without. Ideally you will need to work out together what your children need in terms of clothing and items of furniture such as beds, and share the cost of these.

4. **Child support** Get it clear in your heart and your mind *for ever* that child support payments are not linked to whether or not children spend time with their other parent.

5. **Control** If you are the parent with care, accept that this does not make you judge and jury over your children's relationship with their other parent.

6. **Reliability** If you are the non-resident parent, accept that this does not mean that you can come and go as you please. Your children need your regular company, on time and in a fit state for caring for them.

7. **Your own assumptions about being a good mother** If you are a mother, accept that there is more to your role than being the main carer. Children need their mum to be good at caring, at providing and at having a good time herself. Your children's time with their dad is your time – make the most of it.

8. **Your own assumptions about being a good father** If you are a father, be prepared to be scrutinised a bit – at least at first. You may know that you can do all of the caring jobs but your ex may not, especially if she did most of the caring before separation. Be prepared to accept advice and, remember, asking for help isn't a failure either.

9. **Extended family** Get your extended family in order. Your family is likely to consist of Aunty Joan who thinks what you are doing (in sharing care) is dreadfully damaging to your children or a grandma who thinks

that only mums can care for children properly and dads should be out working. If you are going to share care, tell your respective families what is happening and warn them that you want their support, not their opinions.

10. **Listen to the research** The research results are unequivocal: children do better when their separated parents are able to build cooperative relationships that are flexible and responsive to their children's changing needs. If you are interested in this research, details can be found in Resources.

Family myths

There are no formal lessons in schools on how to be a parent. Our parenting skills are expected to come to us instinctively, and we are supposed to know just what to do and when, right from the very start. Most of the parenting classes that do exist are for those parents who are struggling to get it right. In this environment it is not surprising that so many of us find parenting a little bit scary and wish that there were more lessons on being a good parent that we could access from the outset. After family separation your own and your ex-partner's parenting skills start to come under much more public scrutiny. Little wonder then that so many separated parents experience higher levels of self-doubt about their parenting skills in the early days of family separation than at any other time during their parenting career.

When you are starting to build a separated-parenting relationship, it is useful to consider the ways in which you each think and feel about being a parent. It is also useful to spend some time working out what the conscious and unconscious messages were that you received from your own parents. After all, we learn to parent by being parented ourselves, so it makes sense to start with our first experiences of being parented.

Parenting styles

Everyone has a different parenting style and the chances are that yours is either very similar to that used by your parents or will be almost the exact opposite. This is because we are deeply influenced by the ways in which we were parented ourselves, as well as the positive and negative messages that these gave us. For example, children who experienced their parents as being very strict and uncompromising are likely to favour a relaxed and more permissive style of parenting, whereas children who experienced their parents as being relaxed and permissive will often choose a style of parenting that has more rules and regulations. The problem that we have as children is that we have only one experience of being parented, and we can, therefore, only either draw instinctively upon this and replicate it or reject it and form our own approach. This option, however, is likely to be just as deeply influenced by our parents' approach simply because it is in opposition to it.

To be truly independent and to build a style of parenting that is all our own we need to be aware of the ways in which we were ourselves parented so that we can pick the things we liked about our parents' approach and get rid of the things that we didn't like. From the list that follows, therefore, think about how you experienced being parented and how this relates to your own approach to being a parent.

- **Overprotective** parenting is passive and seeks to calm negative emotions at the first sign. There is often a lack of clear boundaries and an inability to reassure children about their fears. This style of parenting often leads to submissive and dependent children who appear passive but lose their temper if they cannot get their own way.

- **Dismissive** parenting does not acknowledge a child's feelings or fears and aims to push negative experiences away. A dismissive parent will often ignore what a child is telling them and try to distract them with an (usually inappropriate) alternative such as sweets or biscuits. A parent who says 'don't be silly' or 'nonsense' a lot is likely to be a dismissive parent. This style of parenting leads to children becoming withdrawn or conversely leads to a lot of attention-seeking behaviour such as showing off, small accidents or destructive behaviour towards possessions.

- **Permissive** parenting attempts to put children's needs first by being relaxed and easy-going. Unfortunately, permissive parenting can often fail to set the firm boundaries that growing children need in order to learn about themselves and the world around them. Permissive parents accept a child's negative feelings but fail to offer guidance and reassurance or to set limits for behaviour. Permissive parents are often those who are happy to chat in the aisle of the supermarket while their children dismantle the goods on the shelves around them causing general mayhem all around. Permissive parenting can lead to aggressive and anti-social children.

- **Authoritarian** parenting was often favoured by past generations when children were supposed to be seen and not heard. Authoritarian parenting is critical of a child's negative emotions and often ignores or trivialises feelings. It is a style of parenting that favours punishment and restriction of choices. This leads to compliant and 'well-behaved' children who have low self-esteem and confidence.

- **Child-focused** parenting acknowledges the full range of emotions that are experienced by children. It offers reassurance when a child is afraid and clear guidance about behaviour. This style of parenting sets firm boundaries and sticks to them, compromising if it is clear that it is beneficial to the child. It responds to a child's changing needs and recognises that a child is a separate person with a life ahead that will require the emotional and practical skills that can only be learned in childhood. This style of parenting can lead to confident and outgoing children who are capable of understanding and managing their own boundaries as they grow older.

    It goes without saying that child-focused parenting is our preferred approach but we know from our own experience that those people who have enjoyed this kind of parenting are few. Most readers are likely to have experienced a mix of the first four approaches with one or two being the most common style. Also, depending upon your age, one or more may be more familiar to you, with older readers recognising the authoritarian style and those who were children in the 1960s recognising the permissive approach.

Fortunately, due to the work of a number of prominent figures in the world of child psychology, new attitudes to parenting have emerged that enable the combination of the best elements of each to form an approach that sets clear boundaries, empathises and understands and utilises distraction techniques. This provides an approach that puts children's changing needs for guidance and reassurance at the very heart of parenting.

If you have been able to identify the way or ways in which you experienced being parented, it should be possible for you to start to think about your own style of parenting. Can you also identify the ways in which this has developed as a result of the way in which you were parented yourself? Here is an example of how our own parenting is affected by being parented ourselves.

Karol and the broken shoes

A separated dad, Karol, has a four-year-old daughter, Emilie, who lives with him for three days of every week. Karol and Emilie's mum keep getting into arguments about Emilie's shoes that are regularly broken down at the back because Emilie does not undo her shoes before she puts them on. Karol can't understand what the fuss is about because they are only shoes. When he is asked by Emilie's mum if he helps Emilie to put her shoes on he shrugs and says why should he care if she doesn't undo them, they are only shoes after all and not very important in the scheme of things.

Emilie's mum becomes more and more frustrated with Karol's indifference to the issue of the broken shoes and says that he must buy the next pair, which he does. These too are broken at the back within three weeks and Emilie's mum is furious; another argument ensues during which Emilie's mum shouts at Karol, 'Just because you were forced to undo your shoes by your mother as soon as you came into the house, doesn't mean that Emilie should be allowed to break every pair of shoes she owns within weeks of us buying them.'

Karol stops short and thinks about what has just been said. He remembers his mother's cold and authoritarian voice commanding him to take off his shoes the minute he entered the house. He remembers how he felt then and how much he doesn't want Emilie ever to feel like that. Finally he realises that the broken shoes represent his permissive style of parenting that allows Emilie all of the love and warmth that he didn't get but, at the same time, as a reaction to his mother's authoritarian approach to parenting, fails to set useful boundaries; in this case, undoing shoes before taking them off or putting them on. Karol starts to remind Emilie gently that it's a good idea to undo shoes before taking them off and putting them on again. Things get easier. Shoes last longer.

It is important to think about your own parenting style because it is this that you are going to use as a starting point for building a cooperative parenting relationship with your children's other parent. While you are thinking about your own parenting style it is useful for the other parent to be thinking about theirs. Building a cooperative relationship means that each of you must be prepared to compromise while at the same time keeping the things that are most important to you in terms of bringing up your children.

We all start out as parents with visions for our children that can be disrupted for ever by family separation. By becoming aware of the parenting style that you would like to use as a separated parent and the things that are most important in your vision of how your children will grow up, you will be in a better position to negotiate your new parenting agreement and any changes that may be necessary as your children grow.

Later we will examine your personal values and how you

can have a shared-values agenda with your children's other parent. But first we want to deepen your understanding of your own parenting style by taking a look at family trees and what they can offer in terms of uncovering family stories, myths and messages. All of these have contributed to how you were parented and will no doubt still be contributing to the way in which you are currently parenting.

When two parents separate, they leave children in the middle of two family trees, negotiating two sets of stories, two (potentially) very different cultures and two sets of myths and messages. We consider that it is our responsibility, as separated parents, to understand our own family myths and messages fully and those belonging to our children's other parent in order that we help them to negotiate these. Whereas it is difficult for two separated parents to offer children the consistency of messages that come from daily living in the same house, at the very least it should be possible to agree shared values and approaches to key things such as discipline, bedtime and helping around the house.

Consider how difficult it may be for children to internalise a sense of self-control if they are expected to be in bed at the same time every night in one home and are allowed to stay up until they fall asleep on the floor in another. It doesn't matter whether grandad hasn't seen the children because he is working a late shift, or whether you were always up until you fell asleep on your feet, your children need to be in bed at a regular time and it needs to be a routine that is stuck to by both of you. That is not to say that the odd extra hour can't be granted without turning your children into monsters or that bedtime should stay the same from ages of three to 13, but there should be consistency between homes and each family should be asked to support this.

Family trees

Genealogy is popular these days and many people are discovering who their ancestors were and what they did. At the Centre for Separated Families we use family trees to help parents to understand the impact of their own upbringing on their parenting style. We do this so that people become more aware of the messages that were passed to them from their parents. These messages may well have already passed through several generations before reaching the present day, which is why it is important to work out whether or not they are still useful or relevant.

What started out as good advice three generations ago may not have any relevance to current day parenting and may even be considered dangerous. Take, for example, the advice to swaddle a baby from birth; useful, perhaps, in the days when houses were cold and a child needed to be kept warm but bordering on causing dangerous overheating in a baby in houses today which have central heating.

Family trees can be used in all sorts of ways to discover more about family stories, myths and messages and can also be fun to use. However, they can be emotionally difficult as you start to discover and understand more about yourself. In our work with parents we ask each to work separately on their family tree, and then we work with them to help to identify patterns and messages about parenting and children that have been passed through generations. The purpose is to work out what is useful and what is not and to identify an individual style of parenting that has been arrived at from these factors. We then ask each parent to consider the style of parenting favoured by their children's other parent and to consider whether the two are compatible or opposing. The purpose here is to help parents to adapt their own parenting style a little so that a cooperative parenting relationship can be built.

This part of our work with parents can take several weeks and we don't pretend that it is easy. This stage requires each parent to be a little bit more self-reflective and a little bit more cooperative and it can be difficult, but if you have been able to complete some of the exercises in previous chapters, you will be ready to tackle this exercise.

Exercise: family trees

Looking back at your parents' and grandparents' lives, think about the following questions:

• At what age did people get married?

• Did people get married or did they live together or remain single?

• How does your family celebrate weddings?

• How many people in your family are divorced?

• How do people feel about divorce in your family?

• What are the messages about children in your family?

• What are the messages about women in your family?

• What are the messages about men in your family?

• Who do you feel closest to in your family?

• Who do you feel most distant from?

To draw a family tree you will need a piece of paper large enough to contain every member of your family, living and dead, that you are able to recall. To begin with you will draw a simple family tree as shown in the following diagram.

In this family tree we have used squares to denote the men in the family and circles for the women. You can follow our example or choose whichever shapes you like.

The next stage is to begin to fill in the answers to the questions shown above so that you are building up information about your family, their attitudes and messages about family, marriage, divorce and parenting.

When you have completed your family tree you can spend some time looking for repeating patterns such as divorce, early death or other difficult life experiences. You can examine the family tree for the attitudes and messages that are passed from generation to generation and pinpoint those people in your family tree that you identify with most or least and those who have had the most influence on your own style of parenting.

The key thing about this exercise is to be aware that all families are different and that each has its own way of being. There may be difficult patterns within your family tree but remember that there are no patterns that are better than the others, it is not a competition. Looking at the patterns within your family tree, however, can offer you some real ideas about who you are and how you have learned to be the parent that you are.

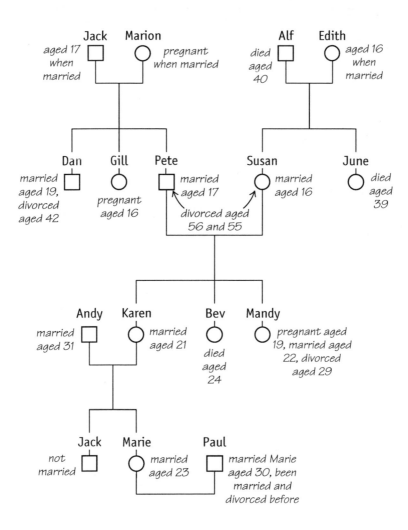

If you are able to swap family trees with your ex-partner this can offer even more insight into the parents that you were together and the parents that you can be apart. This, however, may be too difficult and, if this is the case, try drawing a family tree for your children's other parent from memory, using the things that you can remember and including all of the things that you may have disagreed about. This begins a process of mapping out which of your values are shared and which are not.

Parenting values

The dictionary definition of 'personal values' is that they are your personal standards, priorities and principles. Given that it may be the difference between your own and your children's other parent's values that lie at the heart of your family separation, it might be difficult to understand how you can come to a shared set of values around parenting. But this is one of your goals if you are to build and maintain a cooperative separated-parenting relationship.

When we are talking about your personal values in this section, we are only talking about your principles, priorities and standards as they apply to parenting your children. We are not talking about your personal values in relation to world poverty, recycling or smoking!

When we talk about sharing parenting values we are only talking about the principles, priorities and standards that you wish to apply in your relationship with your children and that you wish to see flourish in your children's relationship with the outside world. We are not talking about sharing your principles, priorities and standards in the ways in which you carry out your parenting tasks. You can still have shared-parenting values even if you disapprove wholeheartedly of the untidiness of the other parent's home or the way in which he/she never irons the children's clothes.

Sharing parenting values, however, makes things easier for children because the messages that they hear from both of you and from your extended family are consistent and easily identifiable to them. Children who have to negotiate two sets of parenting values – often opposing and in conflict with each other – can develop a sense of unreality and a feeling that it is not they who are important in the world but the values that are being imposed upon them.

Finally, it is when children experience conflicting values from their parents that they are most at risk of feeling like possessions, with their allegiance to either party a jealously fought-for prize to prove the rightness of one parent's values over the other. This kind of situation is never healthy for children and they should be protected from it at all times. Remember, you don't have to like the way that the other parent carries out their parenting but you can share similar values when it comes to parenting separately.

Parenting values survey

A good place to begin working out shared parenting values is to think about your own priorities and principles when it comes to being a mother or a father to your children. Think about your relationship with your children, what you hoped for when they were born, what you hope for now and what you might wish for them as they grow older. Think about what you would like them to experience, achieve and understand about the world around them. If you are able to think about the kind of people you would like them to grow up to be, this will lead you to a better understanding of your parenting values. For example, do you wish any of the following for your children?

- Success at school

- Inner confidence

- Contentment with own company

- Popularity with friends

What do you want your children to be like in the world?

- Happy

- Polite and friendly

- Successful

- Wealthy

- Adventurous

- Innovative

What would you say your greatest wish for your children would be?

- That they are happy.

- That they fulfil their potential.

- That they make a positive contribution.

- That they look after you.

- That they are rich or famous.

You will probably find that you are picking out similar words and phrases in the lists above. If you are picking out those words that are related to happiness and contentment then your parenting values are likely to be based upon helping your children to find those things that they enjoy doing. If, however, you are picking out words and phrases that are to do with success and achievement, you are likely to be concerned with schoolwork and academic achievement. Whatever your values are, if they are radically different to those of your children's other parent you may find yourself in a push–pull situation with your children stuck in the middle. Wanting children to do well at school is an admirable parenting value, but when you want that and the other parent wants something else, only your children can lose out in the long run.

In our experience, it is the difference in two family systems, the different messages and family myths and, above all, the different parenting values that create the biggest problems that children living in separated families have to negotiate. If you want your children to grow up with a sense of your parenting values, then be prepared to do some work on negotiating with their other parent just which values are important and how you can support these throughout your parenting time, as well as from a distance.

We cannot emphasise too strongly the danger of forcing your own parenting values upon the other parent. Coming to a shared parenting value system can only be done by negotiation and that requires accepting that you alone do not have the decision-making power about what is right and what is wrong for your children. Unless your children's other parent has a parenting value that is clearly detrimental to the well-being of your children (such as physical, mental or emotional punishment) we do not recommend that you try to force the other parent to conform to your parenting values.

If there is a value that you just can't agree on – for example, one of you thinks that physical exercise is vitally important because it builds adventurous characters but the other doesn't particularly care whether the children are adventurous or not – agree that physical exercise will be that parent's domain and that the other will support it in terms of making sure that sports kit is remembered. Providing the parent who wants the children to be physically active isn't putting them through a two-hour assault course three times each week against their will, this kind of value doesn't have to cause conflict.

Shared parenting values worksheet

At the Centre for Separated Families we use this worksheet with each parent to help them to understand their own parenting values and to help them to negotiate a parenting plan with their children's other parent.

To begin this exercise, make a list of all the things that you admire about the ways in which your own parents brought you up. You are likely to come up with a range of things but try to find the top five things that you feel your parents did well. Perhaps they were:

- Generous

- Easy-going

- Indulgent

- Friendly

- Warm

Don't worry if you can't find five things, just one or two will do.

Now make a list of at least three things that you feel your parents did less well in terms of your upbringing. These things may be something along the lines of:

- Too strict

- Never there

- Always snappy

Finally list at least five things that you like about your own parenting style and how you feel this contributes to your children's well-being in the world; and then list three things that you would like to change. Your final sheet of paper should look something like this:

What you like about your parents style	What you don't like about your parents style	What you like about your own style	What you would like to change
Firm boundaries Clear rules Genuine love Always there Predictable	Strict Uncompromising Firm	Fun Spontaneous Generous Loving Always there	Erratic discipline Passive and then explosive Possibly unpredictable

Those things that you would like to change are likely to be related to the things that you don't like about the way your parents brought you up. This is because, as parents ourselves, we often find that we behave in ways that are the opposite of what we didn't like about being parented when we were children. This often leads to difficulties, particularly if you were brought up by a strict and uncompromising parent and your reaction has been to parent in a free and easy way with few rules and no clear idea of what the boundaries are. The key to establishing strong and positive separated-parenting values lies in finding out what your shared values are and working out how you can come to an agreement about these that you can both stick to.

Agreeing parenting arrangements

By now, we hope that you will be starting to think about the long-term future and in particular the ways in which you will both continue to be parents to your children.

When children are living with a parent on a regular basis it is far easier for them to continue to feel that they are the centre of their parent's world. This is why we would advocate, wherever possible, a cooperative and relaxed shared-care arrangement.

We know from personal experience that this is not always easy to manage but we have found over and over again that it is those children who are able to experience the ordinary, everyday things with each of their parents who fare best. We also know that those parents who are able to be relaxed about arrangements are those who have been able to separate out their own feelings about the other parent from their feelings about their children. We hope that some of the exercises and personal stories in this book, so far, have helped you to work things out so that you can approach your long-term future parenting relationship with your children's needs firmly in mind.

You may already be using parenting phone calls and a more businesslike approach to your parenting arrangements. In this section we are going to talk a bit more about the different approaches that you can take to parenting separately and the positive and negative outcomes of each of these for children.

We will offer a couple of practical tools that we have found to be very reliable for parents who do not wish to see each other or for those who continue to find it difficult to communicate. These are the Parenting Information Exchange Form, developed at the Centre for Separated Families and used successfully with many parents experiencing ongoing conflict; and formal parenting plans, which you can either compile yourselves or use a ready-made plan supplied currently, in the UK, by the Department for Education and Skills (see Resources for the address), solicitors and post offices.

Different styles of parenting apart

Not everyone is comfortable with the same style of parenting apart, and cooperative parenting apart is very much dependent upon your success in overcoming conflict in the early days of your separation as well as the skills you can build for better communication and conflict resolution as you go along.

Successful parenting apart, however, requires one major commitment from each parent and that is that children's needs come first. Success also depends upon each parent's ability to understand that children's needs will change over time and that flexibility will be required on both sides if children are going to get the full benefit of their relationships with each of their parents.

So many parents end up in the Family Court system simply because they cannot accept that their children have the right, as well as the need, to have ongoing relationships with all of the significant adults in their lives; not just the parent with care and their family, but also the non-resident parent and their family, together with all of the connected friendship networks that support each parent. This doesn't mean, however, that children must divide their time equally between their two families and that everyone has an equal right to equal time with children.

In order to grasp fully the ideas that we are arguing for here, it is necessary to let go completely of the idea that parents have 'rights' and accept the idea that parents have responsibilities; responsibilities to ensure that their children's changing needs are responded to as they grow in ways that are age appropriate and child focused. It is our firm belief that the decision to have children is the most serious decision we can make in our lifetime and that from the outset it is incumbent upon parents to put their children's needs first. This is not to say that we believe that parents must be enslaved to their children or that putting your child's need first at the age of 16 is going to be the same as putting them first at aged six. But we believe passionately that being a parent means putting children's needs first and that this is your responsibility for life.

We call our preferred method of separated parenting *co-operative separated parenting* and we believe that this method provides the very best outcome for children.

Cooperative separated parenting

This model of parenting enables each parent to continue to have close relationships with their children that feature regular time together and high levels of communication between parents. Parents who are cooperative will often discuss issues affecting children on the telephone or face to face and will attend school outings or parents' evenings together. Parents who cooperate are mutually supportive and non-confrontational and are able to keep their children's relationship with the other parent separate from their own feelings about the separation. Parents who are able to co-operate are often those who have high levels of skill in communicating effectively and resolving conflict.

Parents in these circumstances have one aim in common and that is to ensure that their children are not disadvantaged by parental separation. Wealthier parents are often better able to cooperate from the outset because the levels of conflict around money and home are lower. This is because parents have the ability to live close to each other and there are no worries about family income or who pays child support and who does most of the caring.

The key quality about parents who do build this kind of parenting relationship seems to be that each is able to recognise that their parenting responsibility comes first and that an ongoing parenting relationship with their ex-partner is both necessary and desirable for children.

Other key aspects of a successful cooperative relationship are:

- An ability to agree and stick to a schedule that suits children's rather than parental needs.

- An ability to share decision-making power.

- A willingness to agree to use similar rules in each household.

- A willingness to support the other parent if things are difficult between parent and child.

Some parenting arrangements are less cooperative but, nonetheless, they can offer children the ongoing relationship that they need with both parents.

Shared-care parenting

This arrangement can be cooperative shared care or formally agreed shared care through the Family Courts. In our experience shared-care parenting that is not cooperative can be difficult for children because of the rigidity of arrangements. These may suit young children who really thrive on predictable arrangements but be far less suitable for teenagers who will appreciate their changing needs being taken into account.

Sharing care of children is often thought of as being half of the week with one parent and the other half with the other. In reality there are many different ways of sharing the care of children, but in our experience these are usually based upon what is considered to be a fair division of time spent with either parent. We have worked with parents who have shared their care of children on a one-week-on/one-week-off routine, a month on and month off, half of the week, and even, where one parent lived abroad, six months on and six months off (with the added benefit that these children became bilingual).

Shared-care arrangements need to be handled carefully, however, and based around what children need and not what parents feel they have the right to demand. There is a growing popularity for a presumption in Family Law that care of children must be shared equally after family separation. This appears to be prevalent among the fathers' movement in the UK with the underlying argument being that this is the only way to ensure that dads are not ousted from their children's lives when the family separates. In our experience, though, this kind of demand misses the point of what children really need, which is cooperative relationships between parents that are responsive to their changing needs.

Children are not possessions to be divided up equally like a record collection and their time does not belong equally to either mother or father. As separated parents ourselves, we know that children do not appreciate being forced to life half-lives so that parents do not feel that they are losing out. Shared care must be underpinned by cooperation and flexibility if it is going to benefit your children in the long run.

Parallel parenting

This is our least preferred method of parenting after family separation but if we had to choose this one over a conflict-ridden relationship we would do. Parallel parenting means that parents rarely talk to each other and do not make any attempt to coordinate household rules. Children living in these circumstances are most at risk of becoming the conduit for information exchange and are also most at risk of being negatively affected by living with both parents on a regular basis simply because of the lack of communication between the two. Parallel parenting means that parents do not have any contact with each other during transition times, which may take place at school with mum dropping the children off and dad collecting them later in the day. In these circumstances, if there is no communication at all between homes it is possible for children to be put at high risk because of the lack of coordinated supervision. Parallel parenting at least means that children live in conflict-free situations but the lack of communication between parents can mean that children feel like they are living in a void. In addition, the lack of conversation or reference to the children's other parent and their life can mean that children feel dislocated and disorientated. Parallel parenting should be considered only if all efforts to build cooperation have failed and conflict remains high.

Agreeing a parenting plan

Parenting plans can be drawn up yourself or you can obtain a template for a plan from the Centre for Separated Families. Parenting plans are useful to formalise your arrangements but in our experience it can take some time to get to the place where you are ready to sit down together and write out your plan jointly. Our advice is to start thinking about the things that are important in your children's lives and jot them down as you are going along. As your arrangements start to settle down into a routine you will notice the kinds of things that might need to go into your parenting plan; there are some examples below of how you might formally write these down. Some people favour each person signing the plan, but in our opinion just having a copy each, along with a list of the things you each need to remember, is all that it takes. If you are committed to cooperative parenting, signing the plan won't make any difference to your input, which is measured by your consistency and willingness to keep at it rather than your signature.

A parenting plan can contain a huge amount of information that you each agree to or it can be pared down and simple. The point about a parenting plan is that it should summarise the key things that you agree to do together as parents and should also demonstrate your shared parenting values. Here are some examples of what a parenting plan might contain.

AGREEMENT ON HOW WE WILL CARE FOR OUR CHILDREN

We will share the care of our children in a way that enables them to be close to each of us. Our children will live with their mother for five days each week and with their father for two days each week. We agree that if there are changes to be made to this routine that requests will be made to the other parent in advance as far as possible. We will however be flexible and in emergency situations we will agree to changes.

COMMUNICATIONS BETWEEN CHILDREN AND THEIR OTHER PARENT

When children are in the care of their other parent they will telephone the parent with whom they are not living at 7.00 p.m. each night to say goodnight. Communication outside of these times should be between us as parents only. As our children get older, we will commit to relaxing these rules and, when appropriate, children will be supported to keep contact with parents as they wish to.

AGREEMENT ON BOUNDARIES/GUIDANCE AND DISCIPLINE

We agree that we will not smack our children and that our discipline methods will be to curtail treats and outings. We will use the 'naughty step' method of building self-control in our children and we will not punish them without explaining what is happening and why. If there are serious difficulties while our children are in our individual care, we will talk to the other parent about these and agree what approach we will take together.

AGREEMENT ON SCHOOL

We agree that our children should attend —— school and that they will not change school without the full consent of both of us. We will each receive information from the school about our children's progress and we will undertake to attend parents' evenings together throughout our children's school life.

AGREEMENT ON HOLIDAYS

We will agree holiday times at the start of each year. Birthdays and Christmas will also be agreed at the start of each year. We will undertake to ensure that our children see each of us on important days such as birthdays and Christmas day, and if this is not possible we will ensure that our children can talk to the other parent.

Using a Parenting Information Exchange (PIE) sheet

Liz Savage (of the Centre for Separated Families) has developed the PIE sheet for the Centre as a way of enabling parents who are still in conflict to exchange information about their children. This can be a useful tool in the early days of family separation when feelings are still raw and it is difficult to communicate effectively. It can also be a useful tool for parallel-parenting arrangements to give each parent the basic information that they need in order to ensure their children experience some degree of continuity between homes and cooperation between parents.

The PIE sheet is designed to be used by email or by post and should be completed by each parent each time the children are moving from one home to the other. It has space for information about health, dental appointments, up-and-coming activities at school and other important events.

We do not advocate sending your PIE chart along with your children, however; this misses the point of it entirely. You should never require your children to carry messages to the other parent, either verbal or written. The PIE chart should not be shared with your children and nor should it be discussed with them. It is for parental information only and neither should it be used to convey any message other than that which is concerned with your children.

Parenting Information Exchange Form

Complete and send this form by email or by post to your children's other parent each time your parenting time is complete. This form gives your children's other parent a clear idea of any issues that they need to know about while your child has been in your care.

Date	Area	Comments
1/10/07	Health	Still has runny nose and didn't sleep too well on both nights. Gave medicine on second night and slept better.
	School	Was not at school on Wednesday as was too ill. Went in on Thursday as seemed better. Sent note to explain absence.
	Behaviour	Was grumpy because of feeling ill but otherwise no problems at all.
	Changes to arrangements	Next week same as usual.
	Other comments/ requests	Could I have the name of the washing powder that you are using so that I can buy the same. I think it's the washing powder here that is causing the itchy skin.
		I would like two tickets to the school pantomime this year if possible as I would like to take Grandma.

If you would like a copy of the PIE chart, please see our website (www.separatedfamilies.org.uk) from where you can download one and start using it immediately.

New partners

As we have said previously the subject of new partners is the only area of our work where we are completely prescriptive. We believe passionately that new partners should not be introduced to children until the relationship is settled and you know that it is going to be long-lasting. Children who have already gone through one experience of family separation do not need to be exposed to the risk of another one too soon.

We also believe that if your family has separated because one of you has a new partner then this person must be kept apart from the situation for as long as possible. We believe that new partners can be deeply detrimental to your ongoing relationship with your children and that it is this relationship that you must continue to put first. In time you will be able to start the process of sharing your life with your new partner with your children but that could be a long time into the future if you have just separated.

So to underline how important we think this issue is, here are our rules for the introduction and inclusion of new partners in your relationship with your children.

New partners – the rules

1. If your family is separating because one of you has a new partner, do not expect to introduce this person into your children's life for a long time.

2. Do not bring your new partner along when your children are spending time with you. You are the person that your children want to see, not your new partner.

3. Do not move a new partner into your home for at least the first year after family separation. This affects your relationship with your children who suddenly have to negotiate their relationship with a stranger as well as their new situation.

4. Your non-parenting time is for your relationship with your new partner so enjoy it.

5. If your children ask you about your new partner or if they suspect that you have one and ask you, tell them the truth but don't compare your new partner to your children's other parent.

6. Your ex-partner needs to know if you have a new partner, show him/her the courtesy of telling them before they hear it from anyone else, especially your children.

7. Always remember that your relationship with your children comes before any new relationship and that being committed to your relationship with your children means that you will have to negotiate your time with a new partner around your parenting responsibilities.

8. If you are a new partner of someone with parenting responsibilities, recognise that his/her children already have two parents and that they don't need another one.

9. If you are a new partner, recognise that you cannot replace the children's other parent and nor should you want to. Your place in the children's life may become important and you can be another significant adult in time, but simply moving in with their dad/mum does not automatically make you another parent.

10. If you are a new partner, accept that your partner is a parent first and that he/she will be communicating and dealing with the other parent for some time to come. Do not allow your own feelings to interrupt the new parenting relationship that is being built.

Conclusion

Your new separated family may feel odd at first and be difficult to come to terms with. What we are advocating is that you begin to build a new relationship with your children's other parent based upon cooperation and continued commitment to your children. This involves coordinating your household rules and your parenting values and agreeing ways of caring for children that are similar. It also involves trying, as far as possible, to communicate effectively and regularly with the other parent and to continue seeing yourselves as a family unit, albeit one that is living separately.

This is not the easy way to parenting effectively after family separation but it is the way that will lead to better outcomes for your children.

Cooperative parenting is somewhat different to many styles of parenting after separation, some of which leave children in a situation where they have to negotiate two sets of rules in two very different households, often with new partners involved. In our experience it is these situations that contribute to children's difficulties in adjusting to change as well as the conflict which can arise when two parents are living very different lifestyles.

Cooperative parenting requires that you are able to set aside your own feelings about the family separation and concentrate upon building routines and ways of living that are similar in each household. It requires that you support the other parent, and value and respect their place in your children's lives. Cooperative parenting is relaxed when it is at its best and parents are not using their children to make themselves feel better about who they are. Cooperative parenting means that you will continue to value all of the things about your children's other family and friends network and that you will be able to talk to your children comfortably about these people.

Cooperative parenting is a lifetime commitment because our role as parents doesn't stop when our children reach the age of 18. Cooperative parenting can turn into cooperative grandparenting when it is successful and then the next generation of children can benefit from the hard work that you have put into your parenting after family separation.

Do not be disheartened with our rules for new partners. We are not saying that new partners should never be involved, what we are saying is that it is important that you take your time over introducing new partners and that it should be children and not they who set the pace. New partners can become very important people in your children's lives, but they will never replace the other parent in your children's hearts and minds.

The most important reason for building a cooperative relationship is so that your children can continue to be close to both of you, those people who are most important to them in the whole world. Valuing your children means that you want the very best for them; what parent doesn't want that? Respecting your children means valuing all that they are and that they have inherited from each of you. Wanting to continue sharing your responsibility to care and provide for your children is key to building cooperation; having the willpower and commitment to keep going even when it is tough means that you will succeed.

Personal Story
Emma and Jean-Paul

My story is a little different as I live in France and I have shared care of my children for several years here in my country. My children's mother lives just 1km down the road from my house and it is, therefore, easy for them to walk between our homes, and if they forget something they can quickly go and get it. My children are aged 14 and 16 now but they were very young when my wife decided that she no longer loved me and wanted to move out of our house. I was very upset at the time, but over the years I have got used to this way of living and enjoy having my children with me on a regular basis.

But this is just a part of my story; well our story, that of my new wife Emma and I. She and I met when I was working in London at the Victoria and Albert Museum. She was curator to an exhibition there and I was reviewing it for one of the newspapers that I write for. She showed me around the exhibition and I asked her if she would like a coffee and we got talking. We soon realised that we liked each other very much (she could speak French which was a good thing as my English then was not good), and we also found out that we were each sharing care of children, which I suppose at that time was not such a good thing because we realised that it would be very limiting to the time we could spend together.

Emma lived in London and was still, at that time, sharing a flat with her ex-husband and their daughter who was aged 12 at that time. The split had been friendly, however, and Emma and her ex-husband were able to share the place quite easily because they had turned into such good friends. I wasn't always comfortable about that arrangement but we felt that it was important that Emma did not take her daughter away from her father at such an age, and I was not in a position where I wanted to leave my children and live in England. So, our children were settled and we did not want to change those arrangements and make them do the moving about, so we decided that it would be us who did the moving about in order to have a relationship together.

For the next five years we spent an awful lot of time on the Eurostar between Paris and Waterloo railway station and vice versa. My arrangements for the children were that they were with me from Friday to Monday during one week, and the following week from Monday evening until Thursday night. Emma agreed with her ex-husband that she would be at home with their daughter on the same days, which left us the rest of the time to spend together wherever we could. In time, we also agreed with our children's other parents that we could take all three children off on holiday together so that they could get to know each other and feel like we were also a family. We spent some wonderful weeks together in different places and somehow also managed to celebrate each of their birthdays together as a family.

After some years of managing our relationship like this,

Emma's ex-husband moved out of their flat and left Emma living on her own with her daughter until she went to university. This meant that I now did most of the travelling, which was exhausting and at times very frustrating. It also meant that we had less time on our own together which was a strain but, thankfully, we had had plenty of time to establish our relationship away from our parenting responsibilities in the early years, which meant that we were able to be strong together. We were both so committed to being our children's parents and we wanted them to be able to grow up in familiar surroundings.

We knew that moving any of them to a new country during their teenage years would be difficult for them, without also asking them to negotiate living in a step-family too. Also, our children were still very close to their other parents and we knew how important it was to make sure that these relationships stayed strong. For me, as a man, it was always a worry to me that if I left France and our regular way of life together, my children would feel that I had abandoned them. Emma's concern on the other hand was that if she brought her daughter to France she would make it hard for her to keep on seeing her father. Our compromise, then, was to say that we would not make any major changes until Emma's daughter was settled at university and my children were older teenagers and more able to cope with change.

I am happy to report that our plans worked out. Emma's daughter is in her second year at university and Emma is coming over to France to live soon. We are going to renovate a cottage close to where I live now so we will still be close enough for my children to come and go as they please (which they do more and more now that they are older teenagers and have lives of their own) and we will have a room for Emma's daughter for whenever she comes over, which we hope will be regularly. Emma will also be able to spend a day in London with her daughter whenever she can as it is so easy to get to England now.

If you ask me whether it has been worth the wait to live with Emma I would say definitely yes, because our children have been so settled and, as a result, we have not had any trouble with them at all. They are each very independent and confident and we all get on very well. It's not been easy to put our lives together on hold for all of these years but we know we have done the right thing in very difficult circumstances. Our way of doing things is not for the faint-hearted but then many people are not in our circumstances. All through it, though, we have been aware of the importance of our children's relationships with their other parents and how it has been our responsibility to support them. We haven't always got on with their other parents but we have always valued and respected their place in our children's lives.

Soon Emma and I will be living together and that will bring its own dynamic as we adjust to life as a stepfamily. But we will be happy to be together at last and to feel like we have given our children all the chances that they need to make a good start in life.

Chapter 7

Our Final Thoughts

WE HOPE THAT this book has given you some ideas about how you might start to build a cooperative relationship after family separation with your children's other parent. We hope that we have convinced you that the benefits to children of doing so are worth the effort that it takes to continue parenting successfully together, even when you are living apart. Our method of building cooperation relies on your willingness to reflect upon your own behaviour, to separate out your feelings about your ex-partner from the way that you feel about your children, and to continue having a relationship with their other parent.

We know that in the current climate of public debate about separated parenting that there is still a long way to go before both parents are valued and supported in continuing their relationship with their children. We know that the continued division of separated parents into one parent who 'cares' and one parent who 'provides' is not helpful, particularly when we continue to associate motherhood with caring and fatherhood with providing. Gender assumptions about what makes a good mother and what makes a good father are always going to be difficult to challenge, particularly because they are reinforced everywhere. We know that mothers and fathers who try to share the roles of caring and providing can find it hard going, especially if their extended families are not supportive of their efforts.

But we wholeheartedly believe that sharing the roles of caring and providing for children after family separation is the right way forward for separated parents. We also firmly believe that we are all capable of offering children the nurturing and warmth of ongoing care and the security of ongoing financial provision. We do not believe that sharing these roles more equally between mothers and fathers takes anything away from either parent. We believe that, for mothers, it adds the benefits of being able to pursue a career or study and eases the burden of expectation that they will take up the majority of care. And we believe that fathers can and will take up the challenge to share the care of children, including the daily tasks of coordinating child care, ensuring clothes are washed and children are fed, along with working outside of the home. We believe that this is the way that children can continue to live their ordinary lives with each of their parents and that each parent's need for support in delivering these outcomes for children should be met by governments and agencies set up to support family life.

We have based our model of supporting separated families on a long history of working with parents and their children. We have developed our Children in Focus courses to support parents to build cooperative parenting relationships, and this book contains much of what can be found on a course. The purpose of writing this book has been to make our support more widely available. You can pick and choose what you need from the book and if you need extra help you can use our website: www.separatedfamilies.org.uk.

Everyone who works at the Centre for Separated Families has personal experience of cooperative parenting. Some of us have used cooperative parenting throughout our children's

lives; others have used some of the techniques that we advocate to build separated-parenting relationships that are as
close as possible to the cooperative model. The key things
about cooperative parenting are that it is child focused and
gender aware, which means that each parent puts the needs
of children first and each is aware of the different experiences
that mothers and fathers have when the family separates.
The different ways that boys and girls experience family
separation are also key to cooperative parenting, and
responding appropriately to these different needs is part of
each parent's commitment.

As authors of this book we have shared between us more
than 12 years of parenting alone using different models of
separated parenting. For the last few years we have worked
hard personally to make sure that our parenting relationship
with our children's other parent has been as cooperative as
possible. We know that it works and, with three children in
their mid to late teens, we see the results in their confidence
and their achievements. At the age of five, all of our children
were statistically at risk because of family separation, and yet
each one has gone on to achieve at school, form strong relationships and have confidence in their ability to cope in the
world. We firmly believe that this is the result of the work we
have done in building cooperative relationships and putting
our children's needs first.

When you face family separation you may feel that you
will never be able to come to a workable agreement with your
ex-partner. The hurt and pain that comes with family separation can feel intolerable and the despair that follows, as you
progress through the process towards acceptance of the
change, can seem impossible to bear. Our advice, though, is
to stay with that process and let the change unfold in yourself. Deal with your feelings and get the help that you need

from your family and friends away from your children. Keep the lines of communication open with your ex-partner and, above all, try to ensure that your children spend regular time with each of you right from the first days after your family has separated. What you do in the early days can be built upon and so it is important that you establish routines for yourself and your children. If all that you manage to do in the early days is make a meal and sit down at the table with your children to eat it you will have achieved a great deal. Things do get easier so keep supporting your children using the ideas that we have set out in Chapter 3. You are hurting, but your children are hurting too and they need you to be able to comfort and reassure them that you can cope. They may be scared that things will never settle down and that they have lost the certainty of their relationship with the two of you for ever. Use any of the tried-and-trusted ideas that we have developed to help you to help your children to cope better.

One day, when you do not feel so raw, you will be able to see how important your children's relationship with their other parent is. Try to keep that in mind, even when you feel so angry and hurt that you just want to stop your children from ever seeing their other parent again. Your children will always see that person as their parent; it can't be changed even if you prevent them from ever speaking about them again. Your children need their other parent and their other family. These are the people who have contributed to who your children are. Try to value and respect that and you will help your children to build confidence and self-esteem for life.

Finally, when you start to work out how you are going to parent together while living apart, think carefully about the things that you want your children to experience as they grow and make sure that your children's other parent is willing to support an agenda for shared values. Coordinating things like bedtimes, school work and discipline can offer your children the safety and security that they need while ensuring that they are not having to negotiate two very different approaches to being parented.

We believe that parenting cooperatively can offer children the safety and security of knowing that both parents love them and that their parents will continue to put their needs first. We have called this book *Putting Children First* because we firmly believe that this is our responsibility as parents living together and as parents living apart. We realise that we have been prescriptive when it comes to new partners, but we know that it's not easy to put your children ahead of yourself when you want to be with someone new; we also know that it is what children need you to do. If you do nothing else but heed our advice about new partners you will give your children something valuable. You don't need to keep your new partner out of sight for ever, but you do need to protect your children from the impact of having to negotiate the dynamics of getting to know a new person while trying to adjust to a new way of living. If you follow our advice for building a cooperative relationship you should find yourself with plenty of non-parenting time each week to spend with your new partner. As a mark of respect to your children, give them the space to deal first with the family separation and the new way of living before you introduce someone new into their lives.

Cooperative parenting is a way of life when it has been properly established. Children know that they can rely on each of their parents to be there, and parents, too, know that they are continuing to contribute to the hopes and dreams that they once shared together when they set out as parents.

Putting children first doesn't have to mean that you set aside the rest of your life or that you do not fulfil your own hopes and dreams. Putting children first means that you consider your children's changing needs, as they grow older, alongside your own. Gradually, when your children reach their older teens, putting them first means enabling them to take more control over their own lives while being prepared to be there as their parent when they need you. Putting children first can enrich your life as a separated parent and give your children all of the things that you hoped to give them on the day that they were born. We hope that what we have offered you in this book will help you to build your cooperative relationship with your children's other parent. Good luck.

Further Reading

Bainham et al., *Children and their Changing Families: Contact, Rights and Welfare*, Hart Publishing, Oxford and Portland Oregon, 2003

Pryor and Rodgers, *Children in Changing Families: Life after Parental Separation*, Blackwell, 2001

Anne Ancelin Schutzenburger, *The Ancestor Syndrome*, Routledge, 1998

Smart and Neale, *Family Fragments*, Blackwell, 1999

Thayer and Zimmerman, *Adult Children of Divorce*, New Harbinger Publications, 2003

Thayer and Zimmerman, *Co-Parenting Survival Guide*, New Harbinger Publications, 2001

Resources

Our resource list contains some of the organisations that we feel can offer you the help that you may need to build cooperative separated-parenting relationships.

There are many more organisations delivering support, separately, to parents with care or to non-resident parents. We have not included those organisations here.

We have given website details for the organisations listed but recognise that there will be parents without internet access. Most public libraries will be able to offer access for free or a nominal charge.

Centre for Separated Families (www.separatedfamilies.org.uk)
Offers advice, information, counselling, parenting support groups and more to mothers and fathers and wider kinship such as grandparents, aunts and uncles to help families build a cooperative separated-parenting relationship.

Citizen's Advice Bureaux (www.citizensadvice.org.uk)
Offers advice and information on finance, welfare benefits and other issues relating to family separation. Find the address for your local branch in the Yellow Pages.

Dads-UK (www.dads-uk.co.uk)
Offers support to dads coping alone with caring for children either because of bereavement or separation. Also offers support in setting up local groups.

Disabled Parents Network (www.disabledparentsnetwork.org.uk)
Offers dedicated support to disabled parents.
Tel: 08702 410 450

NCH – Action for children (www.nch.org.uk)
Provides contact centres for separated families to spend time together where it is not possible to have contact between parents and children in any other way. Delivers support to mothers *and* fathers in ways that meet their different needs.
Tel: 020 7704 7000

One Parent Families Scotland
(www.oneparentfamiliesscotland.org.uk)
We recommend this organisation chiefly because of its recognition that mothers *and* fathers need help after family separation.
Tel: 0808 801 0323 13

Relate (www.relate.org.uk)
Offers counselling for couples who are separating which can help you to address your emotional issues. Find the address in your local Yellow Pages.
Tel: (lo-call) 0845 456 1310 or 01788 573241

Samaritans (www.samaritans.org.uk)
Samaritans is available 24 hours a day to provide confidential emotional support for people who are experiencing feelings of distress or despair, including those which may lead to suicide.
Tel: 08457 90 90 90

AUSTRALIA
Mensline Australia (www.menslineaus.org.au)
Mensline Australia is a dedicated service for men with relationship and family concerns. It offers counselling, information and referral 24 hours a day, 7 days a week. Advice is confidential, anonymous and provided by fully trained professionals; all for the cost of a local call on 1300 78 99 78.

Children, Youth and Women's Health Service (www.cyh.com.au)
This is an extremely useful site for parents provided by the
Children, Youth and Women's Health Service in South Australia. It
is full of helpful advice for both parents covering all aspects of
children's health and development together with support for mums
and dads. Check out the 'being a mum', 'being a dad' and 'single
parenting' links under the 'Family & Relationships' list.

Family Relationships Online (www.familyrelationships.gov.au)
Family Relationships Online is a key component in government
support for building better family relationships. It provides all families (whether together or separated) with information and advice
about family relationship issues. It allows families to find out about
services that are funded by the government that can assist them to
build better relationships. It also provides information on the
government's reforms to the family law system to help families
focus on the needs of their children.

**Department of Families, Community Services and Indigenous
Affairs** (www.facs.gov.au)
The Australian government provides information and support to
help parents whether they are living together or apart. This website
offers some useful information on a whole range of important issues.

SOUTH AFRICA
Family and Marriage Society of South Africa (www.famsa.org.za)
FAMSA exists to empower people to build, reconstruct and maintain
sound relationships in the family, in marriage and in communities.
The website contains some helpful information and support for
those experiencing family separation.

Family Life Centre (www.familylife.co.za)
Family Life Centre (FAMSA, Johannesburg) is affiliated to FAMSA
National Council and is one of the FAMSA organisations in South
Africa. It has some helpful advice through its 'parenting' link
together with a list of counselling services.

Index

Note: Page numbers in **bold** refer to diagrams.